The
world
belongs
to
those
who
can
offer
the
greater
hope.

WHEN ENOUGH IS ENOUGH

David Augsburger

HERALD PRESS
Scottdale, Pennsylvania
Kitchener, Ontario

WHEN ENOUGH IS ENOUGH

Discovering True Hope When All Hope Seems Lost

CARING ENOUGH TO GIVE UP HOPE

The hopes I have for my husband or wife can create or destroy the relationship. (When I love my hopes of what he may be or she might become even more than I love the person that is, the hopes become enemies to us both.)

Caring is letting go of these hopes.

The hopes I hold for my child can invite or inhibit its growth. (When I love my picture of what the child should be or ought to become more than I love the child that is, the hopes betray us both.)

Caring is letting be without such hopes.

The hopes I carry for myself may be freeing, or binding or blinding. (When the hopes I carry for my own future demand achievement, performance, position as necessary for a sense of personal worth, or as entrance requirements for celebrating life as the gift that it is, then they are self-destructive poisons within me.)

Caring is letting go, letting be, letting live.

Most emotional and relational pain in life is caused by holding on to past hopes, or holding back from the future because of false hopes. So the healing power of HOPE is blocked by all the failed and failing hopes that stop us from truly living.

Far from being the joyful, positive, confident feeling it can be, hope is more often a bleak nagging emotion that drains life of happiness for years.

Hopes that fix one's whole life on a desired relationship, a longed for career, a much wanted job, an all-consuming goal can slowly destroy a person's center, erode the identity, destroy the sense of self. The disappointment of hopes is the parent of despair which can drain one's world of life energy, leaving it a joyless place.

Hopes can destroy not only personhood and relationships, it is the enemy of community as well. Dietrich Bonhoeffer has written:

"Every human wish dream that is injected into the Christian community is a hindrance to genuine community and must be banished if genuine community is to survive. He who loves his dream of a community more than the Christian community itself becomes a destroyer of the latter, even though his personal intentions may be ever so honest and earnest and sacrificial."[1]

Hopes must die before Hope is born. Wisdom is gained slowly in life, and much of it comes by at last realizing that enough is enough, the old hopes have outlived their usefulness or are seen at last as useless.

Personal growth proceeds at the pace of our identifying, owning and canceling such self-defeating hopes.

Relational growth occurs as persons become aware of the hopes that separate them in false independence or bind them in immature dependence. Then the growth of mutual, reciprocal interdependence begins.

Pastoral care is the work of enabling persons to

recognize, identify, clarify, correct, and cancel hopes that frustrate health and healing. It is setting rumors of grace afloat in the unconscious that call out HOPE. As HOPE is born, life can begin again.

"Earthly hope must be killed; only then can one be saved by true hope," wrote Danish philosopher Sören Kierkegaard in his characteristic stark honesty.[2] The longer one lives, the more deeply one feels, the more whole one becomes, the fewer the hopes. But those few become all important. For hope is the first and last breath of life.

David Augsburger
Goshen, Indiana
Spring, 1984

Notes

1. Dietrich Bonhoeffer, *Life Together* (New York: Harper and Row, 1954), p. 27.
2. Sören Kierkegaard, *Purity of Heart Is to Will One Thing* (New York: Harper and Row, 1956).

CHAPTER ONE

LOSING HOPE—
REFUSING HOPE
Hopes Lost and Found in Life

I said to my soul,
be still,
and wait without hope,
for hope
would be hope
for the wrong thing.

—T.S. Eliot
East Coker

Hope is a treacherous enemy.

Hope is a trustworthy friend.

Hope sustains the schemes, aims, dreams, and games that keep people waiting, pursuing, circling, seducing, controlling or being controlled. Hope that these old strategies will someday pay off, holds people back from risking, changing, growing, from truly living.

Yet no one can live without hope.

It is hope that heals. Hope is the basic energy of civilization, of social existence, of individual life. One must have goals and the confidence that they can be achieved, and this is hope. Only when there is a genuine basis for hope does growth occur or healing happen.

We move in the direction of our hopes.

And there lurks a danger.

Only as hopes die are we free to live in deeper ways. The high hopes of surface optimism, the hidden hopes of old behavior cycles, the false hopes of our power strategies, or the futile hopes of old conflict responses all must die before hope—healing hope—is born.

The simple hopes of common sense and popular opinion betray us more often than not; and yet that elusive time when they do pay off lures us to renew them in spite of the pain they continue to cause or feed.

As long as there is hope, the addict will pursue his addiction, the drug dependent will cling to the bottle, needle, or powder. The hope that the short-term high will lift the long-term low; the hope that anesthetizing the pain will alleviate the problems; the hope that silencing the symptoms will cancel the cause only sharpens pain and deepens the dependency. Only when hope is lost is hope found.

The alcoholic is someone who says:
"Drinking has cost me my job, my family, my friends, my marriage, and my health; yet I think I'll give it one more try."

The attached child who cannot mature says:
"I've waited for my father's acceptance for forty years. I've refused to believe that anyone else loves me until he comes through with affection. It has ruined my marriage and estranged my own children. Although he's now dead, I think I'll wait for him another ten years."

The resentful person is someone who concludes:
"I've been harboring this anger at those who wronged me for a long time. It has eaten through my stomach, alienated me from others, turned me bitter toward life, and brought me no satisfying relationships, but I think I'll hold on to the resentments a while longer."

As long as there is hope, the rescuing spouse will cover for the alcoholic, tolerate the irritation and abuse, bend the schedule, break the budget, ruin the family plans to adjust to his bender. The hope is irresistible that the most recent promise will be kept, that this new apology will prove genuine, that the latest pledge to go dry will be the last. Only as the hope of saving another from himself is seen as hopeless, can real hope emerge. Only when the hope of supporting the other's cycles until she fulfills her repeated promises is given up, does real hope appear.

As long as there is hope, the grown-up child will continue to search for the rejecting parent. Hope induces the person to keep calling for the father to come and give love, even long after he is dead. Hope seduces the adult to search lifelong for a mother to give her unconditional acceptance, attention, and adulation. Only when these hopes die is hope born.

As long as there is hope, the Don Juan will dream of a more desirable lover, pursue a more exciting liaison, seek "conquest" after conquest. It is hope that lures the woman to look for affection or infatuation outside her covenant of marriage. Perhaps the next lover will have the magic, the mystery, the magnetism that will satisfy her emptiness. Hopes of finding the irresistible other must die before hope of happiness is born.

As long as there is hope, the search, the pursuit, the strategies go on. In time, hope fades. The highs no longer seem high enough, or are too hard to reach. The lows linger longer and leave a residue of despair. So old hopes get renewed. It's painful to admit that "I'll never be able to find a perfect lover, or save the eternal victim, or reform the rebellious

"I hope for nothing.
I fear nothing.
I am free."

—Epitaph of Novelist Nikos Kazantzakis

"Fate is unchangeable
hope is an illusion,
the food of exiles."

—Aeschylus

"Hope is man's curse."

—Euripides

"Hope is the worst of evils,
for it prolongs the torment of man."

—Nietzsche

"Both suicide and hope
are retreats from the courage
to accept the absurdity of life."

—Albert Camus

* * * *

Three things endure
Faith, hope and love.

—St. Paul

"Everything that is done in the world is done by hope."
—Martin Luther

"The hopes we develop
are a measure of our maturity."

—Karl Menninger

For to him that is joined
to all the living
there is hope.

—Ecclesiastes 9:4

child, or revenge the unjust crime." "I'll never get what I must have to survive." "My dream will never come, no matter how long I call or wait or hope." So, rather than yield the vain hopes for a better conclusion, one trusts them to the bitter ending.

Hope may offer patience in times of stress; but it may breed complacency in situations that require change. Hope can inspire action and tireless effort; but it can also be useless activity and wasted effort.

The Many Faces of Hope

"Passive patience" often poses as hope. In fact it may be its very opposite. When the "hope" is a cover for resignation it becomes a kind of "waiting for whatever will be." Drained of all active trusting, choosing, or risking this pale substitute for hope expects nothing in the *now* but all in the *then*.

Franz Kafka has beautifully described this passive sitting and waiting in the parable of the man whose entire life is spent outside the door awaiting permission to enter, never recognizing that the permission of hope must arise from within. Passive waiting is hopelessness disguised as the virtue of hope, impotence masked as endurance.

If Kafka's man had possessed more than this passive waiting hope, he would have gathered strength and entered. The courage to disregard the legalistic bureaucrat doorkeeper and to act by faith and hope would have been the liberating act which would have brought him into the promised palace.

"Determined denial" may present itself as hope. When the shock of tragedy, the pain of injury, the threat of suffering, the finality of death are confronted, one may close the eyes to the approaching

Stories of Hope

Kafka's Peasant

Franz Kafka, in *The Trial* describes resigned and passive hope with this marvelous story of a man waiting outside the door leading into heaven (called the Law).

"Before the door stands a doorkeeper. To this doorkeeper there comes a man from the country who begs for admittance. But the doorkeeper says he cannot admit the man at the moment. The man asks if he will be allowed to enter later. 'It is possible,' answers the doorkeeper, 'but not at this moment. If you are so strongly tempted, try to get in without my permission. But note that I am powerful. And I am only the lowest door-keeper. From hall to hall, keepers stand at every door, one more powerful than the other.'

"The man looks closely at the doorkeeper in his furred robe, with his huge pointed nose and long thin Tartar beard, he decides that he'd better wait until he gets permission to enter. The doorkeeper gives him a stool and lets him sit down at the side of the door. There he sits and waits for days and years. As he grows old he mutters to himself, he begs even the fleas in the doorkeeper's fur collar to help him persuade a change of mind.

"Now his life is drawing to a close. Before he dies, all he has experienced condenses into one question. 'How does it come about then, that in all these years no one has come seeking admittance but me?' The keeper replies: 'No one but you could gain admittance through this door, since this door was intended for you. I am now going to shut it.'"[1]

realities and in the name of hope deny the inevitable.

"Hope can masquerade as the mother of dreams—what could be, should be, might be—but never is. It springs eternal when the world seems to be flooded with grey and death . . . it saves from death and lets people die. It is the last stand of desperation, the false promise of deceit. It is deep in the bones of people, emotional and not feeling or reactive. It is neither reasonable nor unreasonable. It simply is."[2]

"Wishful longing" is frequently misnamed hope. If wishes and desires were hope, then those who long for a better home, a newer car, a desired luxury would be people of hope. But the central motivation of such emotions of consumerism may be greed, or an escape from the present situation.[3]

Through a life of hardship and poverty, many a person has existed by believing in the coming of an inheritance, a lottery, a stroke of fortune that would relieve all fears. Susanna Wesley spent a lifetime hoping that her older brother would return from India with great riches from the colonial exploitations, but "her ship never came in."

Hoping and wishing, as Gabriel Marcel observes, are two entirely different processes. In hoping, one is concerned with a basic confidence toward life, with basic trust in those values that are enduring and eternal—in love, justice, truth, grace. In wishing, one focuses on specific things—needed money, a desired job, a desired victory.

"The hoper tests reality, the unbridled wisher engages in magical thought. The hoper refers and defers to a transcendent power that has its own unfathomable purpose; the wisher bends it down to conform to himself. In theological language, the

Stories of Hope

Ancient Greece

Pandora, the first woman created by the gods was made in heaven, every god contributing something to perfect her. Venus gave her beauty, Mercury persuasion, Apollo music, etc. Thus splendidly gifted, she was conveyed to earth and presented to Epimetheus. Along with all the marriage presents the gods also gave her a box into which every god had put some blessing, but warned her not to open the box except in great necessity.

Seized with eager curiosity, Pandora opened the box without caution, and all the blessings escaped like butterflies. And when she looked again, all had flown out of reach, out of sight. When her tears and sadness had poured out, Pandora heard a faint whisper from the box and opened it carefully once more to find one blessing had remained, the blessing called hope.

hoper is an eschatologist who lets God be God, the wisher is only an apocalyptist, who seeks reversals of his fate in which his revengeful fantasies will be fulfilled to the letter. The hoper says, 'now I see through a glass darkly . . . ' while the wisher cherishes his room reservation in a heavenly motel."[4]

To use an expression by Martin Buber, hope "imagines the real." True hope visualizes what should be for all humankind, since "hope cannot be achieved alone."

"Learned illusions" are the most common form of counterfeit hopes. The expectations that one can control, seduce, placate, or manipulate by habitual behaviors or clever strategies are ultimately found out to be false. Yet these fantasies continue to shape behavior, values, and goals even when they have proved self-defeating or self-destructive.

Overindulgence in childhood can inflate the hopes of being in control of others and motivate such attempts throughout life. Or the direct reverse may occur as emotional undernourishment evokes hopes of someday being loved, valued, approved, or provokes hopelessness about ever being wanted, accepted, or prized. So the illusory hopes, learned early in life, continue through youth, adulthood, and older age.

What Hope Is and Is Not

Optimism is not hope.

Optimism as a constant and consistent attitude is possible only when one has a world view that is highly selective. Continuous optimism depends on a view that eliminates the real evils and contradictions of the world. Chronic optimists look at life with a positive mindset that sees

Optimism
is dependent
on a vision
of future possibilities
considered from
a safe, objective distance.

"If your vision
were as good as mine
you would obviously
see that the future
is positive."

(All relevant factors
have been considered
from the long-term
point of view, and
anyone who shares
this vision will
experience the
same confidence.)

The Optimist is
a spectator.

A doctor may be
optimistic about
a patient's recovery,
but becomes hopeful
as there is personal
involvement and caring.

Hope
is drawn from
a deep intuition
rising from the most
intimate
and living part
of one's inner self.

The hoping person
is personally involved,
like one who loves
another,
or cares deeply
about life.

(Hope does not see
the situation
from the detached,
objective
perspective,
but from the heart,
from compassion
rooted deeply within.)

The hoper is
a lover.

A person who hopes
does so from a sense
of centered integrity
(being true to the self)
and of deep commitment
(being true to another).

everything in the same shade of rose. The habitual pessimist, in contrast, is overwhelmed by a tragic picture of the world and blind to the possibilities that might change or renew the evils that are feared.

One who hopes recognizes the pain and suffering in life, yet sees reason for confidence. Hope is born not from the absence of all that is harsh or sad, it rises from the experience of both good and evil. Hope sees what is possible even in the midst of what is undesirable.

Deep within the optimist, there is an exaggerated "hope," more emotional than rational, that is expressed in feeling statements like: "No matter what happens, it's all for the best; it will work out if I look on the brighter side."

Futurism is not hope.

Total trust in tomorrow as the solution to today's troubles is not hope, it is "magical thinking." A totally future oriented "hope" drains the present of its power and wishfully trusts the future. Futurism longs for what is absent now but imagined for then. Hope is not a yearning for what is unknown, it is a longing for more of what is known; it is not a preoccupation with what may come, it is a concern for increasing and enriching what has begun.

At the center of the futurist, there is the deferred "hope" that tomorrow will solve all problems, resolve all difficulties. It comes through in almost automatic statements: "Tomorrow things will be different. When I'm in high school, or in college . . . or through school . . . or when the children are gone . . . or when I'm financially secure . . . or when I retire."

Egotism is not hope.

Although it often substitutes for it, the only hopes many persons feel are the wishes or desires for reaching private dreams that will advance or enhance their own image of themselves. Hope is more than the anticipation of attaining personal goals. Such expectations serve the self well, but they may contribute little to the meaning of one's life. Meaning arises from commitments to purposes beyond oneself and one's own satisfactions.

At the core of the egotist (a self turned inward on the self) are many hopes that circle around the self. These surface in unconsciously revealing statements: "When I've finally succeeded . . . achieved . . . arrived . . . then I'll have worth, impact, respect . . . "

Hopes of fulfillment of career success, interpersonal relationships, marriage, parenting, and even public service or voluntary service to human need may all be egocentric hopes if they are pursued for one's own gratification. Authentic hope is expressed when one has caught a vision of values that will outlast one's own life, benefit more than one's own kind, and serve those who may have little to offer in return.

Optimism with its fixation on positive thinking, futurism with its romantic hope in tomorrow, and egotism with its self-centered hopes all fall short of real hope. The hoping person will be optimistic, but his or her optimism has the depths of hope beneath it. The hoping person has faith in the future, but the faith has a strong foundation in history, and a solid connection with the present, and therefore confidence in tomorrow. The hoping person has many personal goals that fulfill ego needs, but the self-esteem is rooted in seeing all humans as equally valuable, and their

Stories of Hope

Ancient Hebrews

When the waters had increased over the earth for a hundred and fifty days, God thought of Noah . . . and he made a wind pass over the earth, and the waters began to subside . . . . Noah waited . . . and then he released a dove . . . to see whether the water on the earth had subsided further . . . . She came back to him towards evening with a newly plucked olive leaf in her beak . . . .

God spoke to Noah . . . . "I now make my covenant with you and with your descendants after you, and with every living creature that is with you . . . never again shall all living creatures be destroyed by the waters of the flood, never again shall there be a flood to lay waste the earth."

God said, "This is the sign of the covenant which I establish between myself and you and every living creature with you, to endless generations:

> my bow I set in the cloud,
> sign of the covenant
> between myself and earth.
> When I cloud the sky over the earth,
> the bow shall be seen in the cloud."
> (Gen. 7:24–8:11; 9:8-14, *NEB*)

A dove of hope
A leaf of hope
A bow of hope
A God of hope

needs as equally important with one's own.

The Two Directions of Hope

Hope is both call and answer; it is an answer that rises from deep within to a call heard from the future that is without. Thus hope has both a push and a pull: the push of confidence, the pull of the possible. Hope is both the push of inner urgency and the pull of outer destiny. Hope is a spark of unshakable trust in the soul. Hope is a whisper of undeniable promise from beyond ourselves.

Hope is the push of confidence within. Hope is a part of the core and center of the human being. In health it is alive, stimulating, evoking, empowering the person to venture toward the possible. In unhealth it continues as the one connecting thread of life when all else fades into despair. As the Pandora story pictures, it remains when all else is gone.

Hope is also the pull of possibility, the lure of the future. Hope is the sense of the possible, while hopelessness is the sense of the impossible. Hope calls one into the unknown, to seek and take the next step. Its five basic elements are: What I hope for, which I do not have, though I know it may not be, yet I feel it is possible, and I answer its call.

If hope were exclusively interior, as is often stressed, then the depressed person who has reached the limit of inner resources would be encouraged to search for the spark of hope to rekindle the commitment to living. At such times, the call from without can begin hope again. Though hope lies deeply within at the core of a person, it can also come as a gift offered by the caring received from beyond the self.

Hope then is relational, one-half within, one-

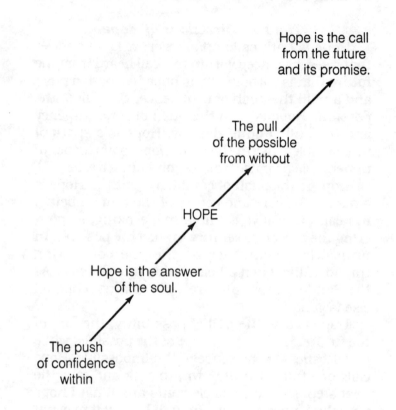

Hope is the call
from the future
and its promise.

The pull
of the possible
from without

HOPE

Hope is the answer
of the soul.

The push
of confidence
within

half without. When it falters within the person it reaches out for its other side on the outside.

This sensitivity to the two sides of hope is deepened by the pain of living. Suffering, though it dashes hopes, may clarify hope. Those who think, feel, and intuit intensely, hope most profoundly.

"In order to hope," writes Paul Pruyser, "one must first have a sense of captivity, of being caught by the human condition. The less life is felt as captivity, the less a person is susceptible to hoping . . . . If reality does not first give us reasons for despairing, it cannot give us grounds for hoping."[5]

Hope rises from pain felt and release desired, from sorrow known and joy anticipated, from injustice endured and dreams of vindication. Both call-from the possibilities envisioned, answer-from the life experience within, and combine in the full-orbed expression of hope.

Hopelessness and Hope

A powerful interlocking set of feelings glue themselves together in the feelings of hopelessness that create despair.

As discouragement mounts, the fears mushroom, the size of the problem seems to fill all available space, the motivation drains away, and energy fades into fatigue.

A sense of impossibility overwhelms the soul. (Nothing is possible, alterable, all is lost.) A feeling of immensity overshadows everything. (All is dwarfed by the demonic threat of the situation.) A conviction of futility permeates all thought. (Everything affects everything; nothing changes anything.) A mood of apathy descends over the whole self. (Who cares; so why should I care?)

I don't know what will happen to me . . .
we've got some difficult days ahead,
but it doesn't matter to me now . . .
I've been to the mountain top . . .
Like anybody I'd like to live a long life . . .
But I'm not concerned about that now.
I just want to do God's will.
And he's allowed me to go up the mountain.
And I've looked over,
And I've seen the Promised Land.
I may not get there with you,
but I want you to know tonight
that we as a people will get to the Promised Land.
So I'm happy tonight.
I'm not fearing any man.
Mine eyes have seen the glory
of the coming of the Lord!

Martin Luther King
Speech to Memphis Trashmen
April 3, 1968.

Impossibility, immensity, futility, and apathy interlock to create a deep sense of helplessness. Whether these are attitudes learned in one's family of origin, or modeled by significant people in one's life, they can well up in times of difficulty to silence the voice of hope within and without.

Hope is a passion for the *possible* that shrinks the immensity of fears back toward *reality,* quickens convictions of some degree of *capability,* and stimulates *activity* to begin in responding even in the smallest of steps. Each of these builds upon the other, each lends strength to the next. A conviction that options exist, an increase in objectivity, an inner response of energy, and an impulse to act, all unite in the emergence of hope.

Hope, as an active dynamic process, is even strengthened by the fear of tragedy or the face of calamity. Hoping is first of all a verb. It is the action that responds to fear with confidence. Hope becomes a noun when the story of and reason for that confidence is later explained and then expressed as religious belief to be transmitted from one generation to the next.

Losing hope, painful as it may seem, is the way to discover HOPE. In refusing hopes we are choosing HOPE. By recognizing the hopes that have betrayed or misled us, we can give them up and discover the hope that is beneath and beyond.

For Reflection in the Bible

The Christian lives by hope, for faith at its core is HOPE.

This hope is described by Saint Paul in his letter to the Roman Christians.

"For I reckon that the sufferings we now endure bear no comparison with the splendour, as yet

Hope

Hope is a combination of intuitions:

Possibility
Hope is the pull of possibility, the lure of the future. Hope is the sense of the possible, and the confidence that it can become actual.

Reality
Hope is a sense of proportionality. Hope is the wisdom to see the difference between fantasy and reality, and to experience both without contaminating either.

Capability
Hope is the core of human strength, the basic central virtue of human existence. In the face of tragedy, hope trusts the power of each action and takes the next step no matter how small.

Activity
Hope is active not passive, venturesome not over-cautious, willing to step into the future integrating trust and risk.

Hopelessness

Hopelessness is a complex of feelings:

Impossibility
"Why knock your head against the wall?" Nothing looks possible, I feel caught, hemmed-in, trapped, defeated. There is no way through, over, around, out. No exit.

Immensity
"It's too big, too much, too bad." The problems are too big to be handled, the fears too terrifying to be faced; Life is too much to be lived. The land is filled with giants, fantasies populate the world with crippling, intimidating, overpowering fears.

Futility
"Why try when nothing changes anything?" There is no reason to continue, no sense in trying again, no goal worth the effort. It is useless to try again, pointless to dream of change, I am powerless to make any difference.

Apathy
"What's the use? What good is it?" The only response to life is to not care, not wish, not get involved. The only way through is to cultivate numbness, passivity, non-action, non-feeling, nothing.

unrevealed, which is in store for us. For the created universe waits with eager expectation for God's sons to be revealed. It was made the victim of frustration, not by its own choice, but because of him who made it so; yet always there was hope, because the universe itself is to be freed from the shackles of mortality and enter upon the liberty and splendour of the children of God. Up to the present, we know, the whole created universe groans in all its parts as if in the pangs of child-birth. Not only so, but even we, to whom the Spirit is given as firstfruits of the harvest to come, are groaning inwardly while we wait for God to make us his sons and set our whole body free. For we have been saved, though only in hope. Now to see is no longer to hope: why should a man endure and wait for what he already sees? But if we hope for something we do not yet see, then, in waiting for it, we show our endurance" (8:18-25, *NEB*).

Note Saint Paul's understanding of the power of hope in the midst of a creation struggling with pain, injustice, despair, and hopelessness. This creation is on tiptoe to see the wonderful sight of God's people coming into their own. This is Christian hope, the hope that all will be set free to realize God's healing and transforming intentions for us. This hope is patient, active, trusting, waiting for what is not yet seen, not yet possessed, not yet received. But hope claims it in faith.

Our faith sets out from hope. Faith is the courage or audacity to act on the premise that all things are possible. It is the daring refusal to regard what is apparently impossible as inevitably or necessarily impossible. So faith and hope are indivisible. Hope, as Sören Kierkegaard maintains, is "the passion for the possible."

"Like faith, hope is the attitude of the adventurer and discoverer, not the technician. Like faith, hope affirms a way out in spite of all obstacles. Christian hope, like faith, is the freedom to decipher the signs of the Resurrection under the apparently contradictory evidence of death."[6]

"The believer is not set at the high noon of life,
but at the dawn of a new day,
at the point where night and day,
things passing and things to come,
grapple with each other.
Hence the believer does not
simply take the day as it comes,
but looks beyond the day
to things which are still to come."[7]

Notes

1. Franz Kafka, *The Trial* (New York: Vintage Books, 1969), pp. 266-269.
2. Thomas F. Fogarty, "The Therapy of Hopelessness," *The Family*, vol. 6, no. 2, p. 57.
3. Eric Fromm, *The Revolution of Hope* (New York: Harper & Row Publishers, Inc., 1968), p. 6.
4. Paul W. Pruyser, *The Minister as Diagnostician* (Philadelphia: Westminster Press, 1976), p. 66.
5. Paul Pruyser, *"On Phenomenology and the Dynamics of Hoping,"* *Journal for the Scientific Study of Religion*, vol. 3, no. 1, 1963, pp. 87,92.
6. James L. Muyskens, *The Sufficiency of Hope* (Philadelphia: Temple University Press, 1979), p. 130.
7. Jurgen Moltman, *Theology of Hope* (New York: Harper & Row Publishers, Inc., 1967), p. 31.

CHAPTER TWO

LEARNING HOPE—UNLEARNING HOPE
Hopes Learned, Unlearned, Relearned in Development

Hope
is
the
basic
ingredient
of
all
strength.

—Erik Erikson

Humanness begins in hope.

True hope supports all that follows throughout the growth of the person; false hopes distort what comes after in the development of personality.

"Hope is both the earliest and the most indispensable virtue inherent in the state of being alive . . . if life is to be sustained, hope must remain even where confidence is wounded, trust impaired."[1]

Hope, once awakened, is the "basic ingredient of all strength." It is the uniting, energizing, exciting force that moves the soul and motivates the will. In the infant, hope is expressed in basic trust of the other; in early childhood, hope emerges in the will to act, the initiative to risk; in school years hope is experienced in learning to perform, achieve, earn, compete, demonstrate competence. Then in youth, hopes are consciously internalized in the formation of identity. Along the way specific hopes that fail us get dropped and more trustworthy hopes are chosen or discovered. At times, worthy hopes are discarded and unworthy hopes retained. The sorting, selecting, and solidifying of hopes is a normal process of growth, and the collected hopes within each individual are a mixed lot, useful and useless, creative and unitive as well as destructive and divisive.

Yet, throughout this entire process, the basic stance of hopefulness toward life that we call HOPE remains, endures all the threats and defeats, survives all the changes and transformations.

Hope—A Gift and a Given

Hope is first a gift, given by trusting and trustworthy mothering. A sense of caring presence is the atmosphere that invites hope. Consistent responses to the infant's behavior, reliable satisfaction of needs, regular affirmation and stimulation compensate for the loneliness and abandonment that fill the hours of infancy. The balance of aloneness and togetherness, of being left on one's own and being held close invite the balance of trust and mistrust that are necessary for hope to emerge as that balanced confidence in what will come. Hope is a gift.

Yet at the same time, hope is a given. The capacity to hope is a part of the basic makeup of the budding human personality. This unconscious hope, rising from the depths of the self is the most primal of emotions in the psyche. As Eric Fromm writes:

"If a tree bends its trunk to the sun, it would not be wrong to say that the tree hopes for sunlight, and expresses this hope by turning toward the sun. Is it different with the child that is born? He may have no awareness, yet his activity expresses hope to be born and to breathe independently.

"Does the suckling not hope for the mother's breasts?

"Does the infant not hope to stand erect and walk?

"Does the sick not hope to be well?

"Does the prisoner not hope to be free?

"Does the hungry not hope to eat?

"Do we not hope to wake when we fall asleep?"[2]

Hope is both gift and given, even as it is both call from without and answer from within. Which precedes which, which initiates which, which is cause to the other is beyond analysis. One is nature, the other nurture at their most basic and

primary level. Neither is sufficient cause, or satis-
factory explanation apart from the other. From the
beginning of life, hope buds in the soul and it is
also nourished by the loving warmth and regu-
lated security of a caring environment.

Hope—From Success and Failure

Hope is kindled by both success and failure, by
comfort and discomfort, by pleasure and pain, by
calm and crisis. It is nourished by constant support; it is exercised and strengthened by difficulty
and adversity.

At some point in life, hopes are dashed, shattered, broken. This is both tragic and necessary. It
is tragic as one is overwhelmed by despair, hopelessness, and feelings of helplessness. It is necessary because strong, resilient, undiscourageable
hope is created only as it is tested, tempered,
transformed. Optimism can mature into hope.
Wishing can go through the complex metamor-
phosis that changes longing into confident expectation.

But hope may be so seriously damaged deep
inside the self that the person cannot tolerate the
recognition of the despair within. One can cover
this dread against the future by adopting the
hopeful optimism of shallow cheerfulness. If all
about whistle in the dark, then it is easy to whistle
along, even though off key. This resigned and
unquestioning sort of positive thinking is devoid
of real feeling. Rather than feel the depths of hopelessness, such persons may shut the inner doors
to the soul. False hopes rise to replace the true. "If
no feelings are recognized, they will never be hurt
again. If no one can come close, they will not be
found out, or betrayed, or abandoned." So hopes

become mixed. Exaggerated hopes with inflated promises; deficient hopes with chronic despair; misguided hopes of self-defeating strategies may be intertangled in the expectations acquired from infancy to adulthood.

Fulfillment of one's hopes confirms their reliability, but failure of one's hopes can reaffirm their necessity and desirability. Both experiences lead to successful growth. The collapse of mistaken hopes, the puncturing of swollen hopes, the exposure of timid hopes can shape and form authentic hope.

Failure of the false hopes that are learned along the way toward maturity can reveal their invisible snares. Success of trustworthy hopes can clarify and correct these most basic views that shape our vision of life.

The Snare of Hope

How dare one speak ill of hope? It offers the last breath of encouragement when all other courage has vanished, the last strength when external supports have failed.

It is not the strength, the courage, the endurance that hope offers that must be examined; it is the wisdom within the hope that must be weighed, the direction of the hope that may require correction.

Hope holds many snares. The deceit of hope can mislead the unwary, and in its search for significance reach insignificant ends.

The snares of hope may snatch the hoper from either side, with over-stimulated expectations or by over-attention and over-stimulation.

Over-hope, inflated throughout childhood, nourished with escalating expectations in youth

The Path of Hope Has Many Snares

1. **OVER-HOPE**
   "All will work out perfectly."
   Inflated hopes of personal
   power, privilege, grandiosity,
   vindictive triumph.

MATURE HOPE

PRIMAL HOPE

2. **UNDER-HOPE**
   "Nothing will work out satisfactorily"
   Deficient hopes of personal powerlessness,
   worthlessness, failure.

3. **MIS-HOPE**
   "I can work anything out my way."
   False hopes of controlling power,
   manipulation, subterfuge.

4. **FAILED HOPES**
   "I give up on hope, any way will do."
   Cheat on hopes, betray hopes,
   spite hopes deliberately.

can exaggerate the hopes of personal power, the illusions of individual grandeur, the fantasies of great interpersonal success. It must, through pain and disillusionment, be tempered by reality.

Under-hope, shaped by a deficit in caring, contact, support in early years leaves deficient hopes of personal powerlessness, worthlessness, and the uselessness of making efforts for change. Self-depreciation, self-fulfilling prophecies of failure, self-negation result.

Mis-hope, misdirected by the fears, fantasies, and false hopes of the family milieu, elicits dreams and drives that are as varied as are families—mis-hopes of gaining power, or of seizing control or of gathering the means of manipulating others to gain whatever is wished.

Cheating on hopes is the fourth snare that hope offers. When hopes are too high, one may seek to reach them by devious means. If they are too demanding or impossible, one may turn them into self-demeaning feelings of helplessness and hopelessness. If they are too costly, one may look for bargain means to reach desired ends.

With all its inevitable confusions, hope is still the central growth stimulus from earliest infancy to the final stages of adulthood. From stage to stage, hope takes successive forms. True hope is mixed with false. Impossible hopes spring up from the strong firm hopes that sustain life and growth.

Hope, once established as a basic quality of experience, remains independent of the "verifiability of hopes, for it is in the nature of maturation that concrete hopes will, at a time when a hoped for event or state comes to pass, prove to have been quietly superceded by a more advanced state of hopes."[3]

Stage 4
FAMILIAL EDUCATIONAL HOPES
(Performance promises made
to self and significant others.)
If I really produce, I am worth something.
If I try hard I can be perfect.
If I am pleasing enough, clever
    enough, successful enough,
        I will always be liked.

Stage 3
CHILDHOOD HOPES
(Moral hopes that you choose before you choose.)
If I am good, nothing bad will ever happen to me.
If I am bad, I get noticed.
If I make myself feel bad (guilty) enough I won't do bad things.
If I say I'm sorry, they have to let me off the hook.
If I don't get caught, it really doesn't matter.

Stage 2
INFANT HOPES
(Emotive hopes that
you know before you know.)
I will get whatever I need
    (If I cry, please, placate)
I can get whatever I want
    (If I demand, pout, shout)
I can be who I am and be liked.
If I hide who I am I am liked.

Stage 1
PRIMAL HOPES
(Intuitive hopes that
you feel before you perceive.)
There will always be a loving
    parent to meet my needs.
Someone will be there when needed.
The world is safe, and the universe friendly.

Primal Hopes (Stage One)

Primal hopes form the "cradle of faith" that envelops, protects, nourishes, surrounds the infant in an emotional womb of love. It is the basis for faith-capacity throughout life. These are intuitive hopes that you feel before you can perceive feelings.

Hope springs within from the moment of birth. It is the primal virtue, the first learned emotion that sustains one across the long loneliness of pre-verbal infancy. Before there are words to reassure oneself that the mother will return, that a face will smile, arms will enfold, the breast will be there again, there is hope rising from the earliest experience. For the abandoned or deprived child the absence of care leaves an emptiness that warns, threatens, hints of famine to come.

"There will always be a loving parent rushing to answer my call, to meet my needs, to fulfill my wishes." This primal hope can remain alive within us as a lingering dream, an impossible dream. It is the core conflict of many neuroses. Or it can be reshaped into the mature form of an intuitive confidence in the trustworthiness of human relationships. The innate intuitions—that someone will be there when needed, that the world is a safe place, the universe ultimately friendly, and life is to be accepted as a gift—all rise from the core convictions of the earliest layers of learned hopes.

This hope generated in infancy is described by Erik Erikson as "the enduring belief in the attainability of fervent wishes in spite of the dark urges and rages which mark the beginning of existence."[4]

Infant Hopes (Stage Two)

The infant years evoke the secondary, emotive

hopes that one knows before one knows. In the second and third year of life, autonomy becomes centrally important. (Have you baby-sat for a toddler recently?) The sense of will emerges as the pampered child overextends in willful behavior, or the threatened child submits in will-less intimidation. When support and control are offered in balanced genuineness, a willing child that is both cooperative and assertive reaches out to others in sensitive and spontaneous play.

Willful hopes can predominate: "I can get whatever I want if I demand, angrily pout, shout"; or, "I may get whatever I need if I please, placate, passively pout or cry."

Will-less hopes can overwhelm: "If I never even think of resisting the giants (the authorities), and never incur the wrath of the powers (the omnipotent/omniscient parents) all will come to me if I quietly, cutely wait."

These hopes will energize the basic life-style to follow. The willful hopes direct the formation of the more irritable personality styles: the aggressive independent authoritarians, the negativistic critics or censors, the angry avoidant suspicious persons are all expressing coercive hopes. The will-less hopes command the more subtle personalities: the conforming saintly pleaser, the winsome attractive model, the clinging dependent joiner, the persuasive flirtatious butterfly all respond to seductive hopes.

Maturity unfolds as authentic hopes motivate the personality. "I can be who I am without fear and be loved for what I am without pretense." "I can ask for what I want and be heard; I can respond to those in authority without doubt of my right to ask or shame for having done so."

The Case of Jill

Jill had never lived in a neighborhood that she liked, had divorced twice, changed jobs almost annually, felt rejected and betrayed by friends, was constantly irritable, yet lonely and longing for friendships.

Childhood began painfully for Jill. An unwanted child, her parents married resentfully to make her birth "legitimate." Although the marriage continued, "It was a living hell for both my mother and me. I was very close to her, very distant from my father. I was clung to, smothered with a superabundance of love and attention. It was like she and I stuck together to protect ourselves from his anger. My father punished me for any fancied disobedience, he was antagonistic to me from the first, since I represented the cause of all his miseries."

The constant total care and affection that Jill received grew more intense as the marriage worsened. Then a second child, a son, was born when she was three. As the mother's attention turned to the new infant, Jill felt abandoned, and all her attempts for attention met with short-lived success. She tried desperately to distract her mother from the brother and recapture her love and protection. This provoked as much annoyance as it did affection.

A lifelong pattern of striving for attention and demanding loyalty while expecting rejection and responding to any imagined slights with intense defensiveness made relationships extremely fragile and tenuous for Jill. Her intellectual brilliance and stunning physical attractiveness won her a succession of brief but explosive relationships.

The over-hopes of constant total support and absolute acceptance, and of her ability to command such loyalty, were exaggerated, in the first three years.

The under-hopes of consistent rejection by her father and of competition with her brother led to a deficit in confidence in males and in herself.

The mis-hopes of manipulating others by use of self, of strategies, of game-playing with others' emotions to draw them into interlocking with her own.

Childhood Hope (Stage Three)

The childhood hopes are directed by a new force, the internalized parent we call conscience. The moral process of choosing the better has begun, although these begin as options you choose before you truly choose. The split between good me and bad me, begun already in the preceding stage, now becomes internalized in the divided will as the child becomes capable of both love and hate, guilt and anger, affection and resentment, at the same time.

"If I am good, nothing bad will ever happen to me," awakens hope in obedience and conformity. A lovely hope, but it is a false one which will soon be disillusioned as one discovers that goodness does not guarantee safety and security.

"If I am bad, I at least get noticed and that is better than being ignored," arouses hope in resisting authority. Such an angry hope settles early for a desired good with a high cost. It will need to die before cooperation can begin.

"If I make myself feel bad enough (guilty) I won't do bad things again" persuades the child to hope in the preventative power of guilt. Later, this hope will have to die, since guilt is a temporary solution that boomerangs.

When guilt is added to guilt, it evokes unconscious resistance and resentment that in turn motivates the old problem once again. Real hope resides in the will, in the willing choice of the better.

"If I say I'm sorry, they have to let me off the hook," invests hope in a whole range of responses from simple apology to exaggerated groveling. In time, this hope too must end. Real reconciliation is not a matter of magical words or ritual acts.

The Case of Alan

"I was just fired," Alan says, sitting stiffly in his chair, his face void of emotion, exhaustion in his tone of voice.

An engineer, Alan had been the head of his division for seven years, but changing production needs, new technology, and the threat of younger, better-educated staff had slowly immobilized him until he was no longer able to function.

An extremely methodical, conscientious, disciplined person, Alan had alienated fellow workers through his rigid demands and legalism on schedules and procedures.

The second of two sons, Alan had followed his father's career as an engineer. His brother had gone into education like his mother. Both parents were "efficient, orderly, and strict." Their life had been well planned, with nothing left to chance. All responsibilities were posted on the kitchen bulletin board. Both sons had learned early to conform to their parents and to the grandmother who did most of the child care. They had early learned exactly what was required of them and knew that punishment would be swift, exact, and unyielding if they failed to meet all expectations.

Alan was a "good boy." Unable to compete with his brother's athletic and social skills, he became a "paragon of virtue." By being scrupulous, orderly, utterly prudent he could avoid any difficulty with his perfectionistic parents. He conformed religiously to their expectations, took their guidance as final, exhibited no anger, internalized guilt, sought to earn approval by always appeasing authorities above, and being strict with anyone beneath.

"I wonder what's the point of trying," he says absently, "I've done all I can to be a good employee, and look what I get."

Over-hope in conformity, conscientiousness, and will-less obedience.

Under-hope in willing choice, responsible autonomy, personal integrity.

Mis-hope in deference to authority as the solution to life threats, and the exercise of legalistic authority as the resolution of life conflicts.

Hope will continue to reside in making things right between adversaries.

"If I choose to trust both the warnings of my conscience and the excitement of my urges, to play safe and to play dangerously, to obey and to explore, to resist and to surrender, then my hopes become centered, stable, trustworthy."

School Years Hopes (Stage Four)

As the child leaves family security to explore peers, playground, and school, the hopes gathered at home get tested against the puzzling differences of other values and views. The hopes learned in the early years are challenged, contradicted, or confirmed. The new pressures that emerge are for performance. Now that the child can produce in measurable, rewardable or rejectable form, new hopes are lifted, or dashed.

"If I'm good at what I do, I am good. If I'm not, I'm a bad kid." The identification of person and produce is a natural expression of the concrete thinking processes possible at this age. If it is reinforced by parents, peers, teachers, the hopes become even more binding.

"If I really produce as expected, I'm worth something; if I don't, I'm hopeless." As grades go up, so does the earliest form of earned esteem. But the child does not feel good about him/herself, he feels good about his produce, she feels good about her performance. Far from being one and the same thing, self-esteem and work-esteem may exist side by side with no transfer. Hope in produce is a false hope. Worth is experienced from relationships where worth is seen, appraised, and honored by the significant persons in a person's life—apart from good the grades, great achievements, and

The Case of Carl

Oldest of three, the only son, Carl was closely attached to his mother, distant and mistrustful of his alcoholic father. As the parental relationship faltered, the mother-son bonds grew more close. At fifteen he was her support, her confidant, her protection when the husband's explosive rages were ventilated on her.

In the middle of the night he awoke to hear them fighting; he heard her call. Breaking into the bedroom he saw them fighting over the father's handgun. Seizing a chair, he struck the drunken man, knocking him unconscious.

The marriage ended that night. The father did not return. The son now became the man of the family with all the responsibilities for emotional support for a dependent mother and two sisters struggling to enter teenage years in a fragmented family.

Carl became a much more complex personality in the next five years. A conforming good boy, with the hope of earning approval through compliance, he became an exaggeratedly responsible young man with hopes of being son, brother, father, provider of all the emotional needs of three others; yet he was starving himself. The hopes that he could somehow take away the pain in the other three people, make them as happy as if none of the tragedy had happened, became the central motivating goal of his working. And at night he sometimes dreamed that he could be the link that would bring mother and dad together again. If he could confront in just the right way, perhaps dad would change, see everything with different eyes and undo all.

Hope upon hope. From the hope of conforming, to overhopes of perfect performing, to mis-hopes of transforming an entire family tragedy, Carl is driven by a compelling goal that is consuming him.

matching of others' prescriptions.

"If I try hard enough, I can be perfect. If I don't and if I'm not, I'm worthless." The dream of being pleasing enough, clever enough, successful enough to win a permanently secure place in the world seems possible enough when one is ten, and by then the dream may be so internalized it is no longer available for review. Driven by such hopes, a man may work endless hours, sacrificing personal life to achieve professionally. Drawn by such dreams a woman may invest her energies in career to the exclusion of time for personal and relational growth. The dreams of perfection and high proficiency, buried deeply in the unconscious and burned deeply in the conscience can direct a life without a pause for self-examination.

Maturity frees a person from bondage to unevaluated hopes only when the false hopes of the first decade are reassembled in the formation of identity in such a way that the personal values affect and direct the whole person with that flexible consistency we call integrity.

Hope Shapes Identity (Stage Five)

As identity forms in the second decade of life, the hopes collected in the first four periods of growth are reexperienced. The central questions of personhood recapitulate the problems already solved, yet at a deeper level. The answers rise from the hopes that have been learned, stage by stage.

The sense of "I-ness" that marks the emergence of identity is grounded in the hopes of being an autonomous self. The feeling of "we-ness" that makes friendship possible is rooted in the hopes of finding trustworthy relationships. The values of "rightness and wrongness" are based on the early

Central Issues of Personhood

WHO AM I?
 CAN I DEFINE MY IDENTITY?

WHAT DO I VALUE?
 CAN I CHOOSE WITH INTEGRITY?

AM I TRUSTWORTHY?
 CAN I ACT, WORK, DRIVE, LIVE RESPONSIBLY?

AM I VALUED?
 CAN I BUILD LASTING FRIENDSHIPS?

WHO ARE MY COMMUNITY?
 CAN I KEEP FAITH WITH FAMILY, PEERS,
 COMMUNITY?

HOW AM I SEXUAL?
 CAN I BE FEMALE/MALE WITH COMFORT AND
 AUTHENTICITY?

BENEATH EACH ISSUE LIE THE PRIMAL HOPES

Can I be me?	(The hope of autonomy)
Can I choose?	(The hope of morality)
Can I will?	(The hope of competence)
Am I liked?	(The hope of acceptance)
Am I alone?	(The hope of fidelity)
Am I sexual?	(The hope of intimacy)

The Case of Ann

Ann is a sixteen-year-old woman struggling with who she is, who she wants to be, who she is now choosing to become.

Four years older than her only sister, Ann has felt loved by both parents, although her father had little time for her; her mother was an emotional yet charming woman who set a high value on her daughters being beautiful and talented. The two girls vied for their father's approval and sought to live up to their mother's expectations to earn her pride and esteem.

Ann was very popular during her junior high years with a lot of attention and affection from the opposite sex. She was editor of the school paper, sang in the fall musical, made the honor society.

Her father has encouraged her to become a doctor, her mother thinks she would be happier as a teacher. Ann is unclear about her own goals, but favors medicine.

Recently she has been plagued with a sense that her life is just "play-acting," that her relationships are hollow, that she is dissatisfied with being who she is. All these years she has made top grades to earn her father's approval, and he simply raises the standard, pushing the goals even higher. Since she was a small girl she has sought to make a good impression on everyone around her, but now she wonders if they admire only her image, not her.

Shall I go on accepting the identity of "daddy's good girl" or of "mother's stunning daughter"? If I choose to be someone different from these, who am I? Who will I be?"

It is the nature of hopes that they must be tested, the over-hopes (conformity, performance) softened; the under-hopes (autonomy, fidelity to self and others) strengthened; the mis-hopes (acceptance through charm and sweetness) mistrusted, corrected. So Ann may move from a second-hand identity to become her own centered person.

hopes of justice, fairness, and goodness. Now, more fully grown, these hopes appear in the choices made and the directions taken as the person is consciously forming a self.

False hopes and true hopes, deceitful hopes and trustworthy hopes are mixed together at the core of every person. Sorting hope from hope is the continuing work of maturation. True hopes that may be expressed clearly in speech are frequently blended with false hopes that are never put in words. The conflicted hopes may struggle for dominance within a person without the source of the contradictory feelings ever coming to awareness.

The mature adult identity is a rich tapestry of hopes, light and dark, clear and blended, simple and confused, woven into a unique flow of patterns unlike any other. True hopes are shadowed, or at times overshadowed, by the false.

Empty Hopes

Most persons come to the time of identity formation with the hungry hopes of emptiness, looking for something out there that will fill (we say "fulfill") or complete (we say "excite") or give meaning (we say "interest") to our lives. Such emptiness evokes a desperate dependency, an urgent search for satisfaction (we speak of as "it").

The "it" may be a place on the football team, the chance to pitch, a headline or a trophy. "It" may be finding the most chic girl or attractive guy, the sleekest car or the most prestigious college. Later it may be a career, a profession, a position. The list of "its" is endless.

Beneath it hide the hopes that multiply in emptiness.

"Perhaps I will find someone who will love me

AS IDENTITY FORMS
(THIRTEEN TO EIGHTEEN)
HOPE TAKES SHAPE

IDENTITY HOPES: "If I accept myself as the person I am, I will be equally accepted/respected by others."

(False hopes: "If I can become my ideal self, not my real self, perhaps others will accept me. I might even accept myself.")

FRIENDSHIP HOPES: "If I reach out to others in friendship, they will respond with equal warmth."

(False hopes: "If I am a winner in everything I do, then others will like me; if I never risk I won't be rejected.")

FIDELITY HOPES: "If I keep faith with my family, with my friends, with my community, with God, I will experience peace within and peace between self and others."

(False hopes: "I can fool my family and friends; I can ignore the community, forget about God and I'll get along just fine.")

RESPONSIBILITY HOPES: "If I can manage time, money, resources, work, driving, I will find I can manage most of the other decisions and directions of my life."

(False hopes: "I need someone to schedule my time, budget my money, oversee my work, police my driving, so that I don't need to worry about accountability.")

SEXUALITY HOPES: "If I can appreciate my own sexuality and experience it as good, I will neither exploit it nor avoid it, neither use others nor abuse relationships, neither devalue the body nor worship sensuality."

(False hopes: "Sexuality gives power over others to attract, control, manipulate; sexuality defines who a person is, what a person is worth; it is the why of existence.")

INTEGRITY HOPES: "If I choose values that are trustworthy, they will guide me lifelong."

(False hopes: "There are no lasting values; one can pick the better in each situation.")

unconditionally, someone to give me attention without evaluation, someone who will be there no matter what choices I make or actions I take."

"Perhaps I will be able to achieve the impossible, pull off some heroic success, hit some streak of luck, or fall into the graces of some benevolent hero and the emptiness will all be filled.

"Perhaps I will find an all-consuming passion, or a total religious experience, or an utterly releasing mystical union, or discover the perfect community of people and will be totally happy."

Empty hopes press toward empty solutions. We are not filled by a fortuitous discovery, heroic achievement or overwhelming experience from without. The empty searcher is hoping for the hopeless. As the Hebrew proverb expresses it, "It is like the fish swimming in water, seeking water," or the Chinese Koan, "It is like a man riding on an ox in search of an ox." Or the African wisdom, "Can the mountain hide its highness, the desert deny its dryness?"

Emptiness is at the center of our humanness. To flee it is to miss the creative openness toward creation and the Creator. To stuff it full of things is to block our ability to receive others in listening love. To anesthetize it with addictive experiences is to deaden the creative springs of the true self.

Substance addictions numb awareness so the emptiness is temporarily silenced; work addictions overcrowd the schedule so the emptiness is forgotten; addictive love attaches the person parasitically to others so the emptiness is masked; addictive religion floods the mind with cyclical superspirituality so that the emptiness is submerged; addictive depression can blanket the inner emotions with fears of the emptiness and

False Hopes

I am empty, hungry,
unfulfilled.
Somewhere there is
something or someone
that will fill me, who will
complete me,
that will satisfy me.
I must find "it."
What I am is not enough,
What I have is not
enough,
What I can now
experience is not
enough.
I am looking for "it."

Perhaps I will find
someone
who will love me
unconditionally
and take the emptiness
away.

Perhaps I will be lucky,
fortunate,
wholly admirable or
heroically successful
and the emptiness will
vanish.

Perhaps I will be
blessed by faith,
or fulfilled by religious
"experience,"
and the emptiness will
be filled.

Hope

There is no "it,"
no magical release,
no instant solution,
no final satisfaction.
Life is to be embraced.
Love is to be shared.
Grace is to be received.
I am loved, as I am.
What I am is enough.

Grace is in the
emptiness,
in accepting the fact
that you are accepted,
even the parts
that seem unacceptable;
in experiencing,
appreciating,
celebrating
that acceptance
for who, what, why
you are apart from
accomplishment or
achievement.

grieving for its presence.

Emptiness is to be embraced as a gift. Emptiness, like all space, is three dimensional: one, as openness to others and the breadth of relationships; two, as openness to the self and the welcoming of depth in wonder, awe, and waiting; and three, as openness to height, to the transcendent, to God, to the upward call of the Spirit.

Emptiness is to be received as a gift of grace. Grace lurks in our emptiness. As we make peace with the open void, the incompleteness within, it is completed by the grace that accepts even our unacceptable parts, appreciates even those sides of the self we have sought to extinguish. The emptiness too is precious. Real hope lies in the discovery that I am graced not because, but as I am; not because I am successful, achieving, earning, meriting and all that, but as I am.

Winsome Hopes

Every person enters the identity crisis of youth with the many unfinished attempts to win the security of unalloyed approval from significant others.

"If I can be what you want me to be, become what you dream for me, perform what you demand of me, surpass what you expect of me, I will have measured up to your standards, and you will love me, forever."

This is the dream of the conforming personality, of the Adam and Eve in idyllic innocence with the simple instructions to go, obey, care, and multiply in the garden of delights. Then the cynical serpent hints of a resistance that lurks within. The rebellion then rises, if only in thought, and the garden is invaded once again.

False Hopes

If I can appear attractive
enough,
seem pleasing enough,
act nice enough,
I will not be ignored,
neglected.
I will not be excluded,
rejected.
I will never be left alone.

(I must be with others
I can't stand aloneness.
I need human support
Or I cannot survive.)

Hope

To be known as I am
and respected as such,
to be seen strong and
weak
And valued as both
is my hope for myself,
my wish for others.

(I value both support
and separateness.
I want both solitude and
solidarity.
I can face my loneliness
And embrace my
aloneness.)

False Hopes

If I can be
what you want me to be,
If I can meet
what you expect of me,
If I can perform
as you demand,
If I can measure up
to your standards
You may love me.

Hope

If you really see me
as I am,
If you really know me
as I know myself,
If you really understand
me
as I want to be
understood,
You will love me.

"If you knew what I'm really like, sensed what I sometimes feel, suspected what I often desire, if you understood what is actually within me, you wouldn't love me."

The false hopes of appearing attractive enough, of seeming pleasing enough, of acting nice enough are flawed hopes. Yet they are powerful enough to motivate persons lifelong. The unfinished dreams of earning approval through yielding, if never examined, can drive one to hope in performance, hope in achievement, hope in production, to be totally, utterly winsome.

Real hope lies in neither compliance nor defiance, on neither eager conformity nor constant nonconformity, but in authenticity, in claiming respect for the self I am which can both resist and surrender, yield and rebel, be both soft and firm.

Relational Hopes

As identity forms, the sense of "I-ness" deepens, the awareness of others' "you-ness" sharpens, and the concern for sustaining a lasting "we-ness" grows. Fidelity is the outcome as one learns to keep faith with others without loss of self or violation of the other.

Hopes of fairness, hopes of justice, hopes of mutual responsibility all mature as persons discover how the give and take of friendships function. Here the unfinished false hopes of childhood can flourish.

"Perhaps I can pin the blame on the situation, or fix responsibility on the other person, or define the problem as unavoidable. Then I am off the hook." The rich vocabulary for delegating responsibility that most of us learn early in life comes to our rescue.

False Hopes

It's not my fault
(The situation made me
do it).
I'm not really responsible
(The circumstances
caused it).
I am not to blame
(The other person asked
for it).
I had no other choice
(There, I'm off the hook).
I hope you will learn
from this,
mend your ways.
Change your behavior.
Stay off my toes
So we can get along
better.

Hope

I can make my own
choices
(In any situation).
I can choose my
responses
(In any circumstances).
I am response-able
(Whatever the other
does).
I have a choice
(That's the "why" of
hope).
I can learn from my
errors,
grow from my failures
By owning my part
In our two-person
problem.

False Hopes

Someday he will "get
his."
Sooner or later she'll
suffer.
     I've gotten a rotten
deal
     I've been cheated,
abused, ripped off.
     May God get you . . .
     May you get yours!

Hope

My hope for myself
is to act justly, fairly,
to live genuinely, freely.

My hope for the other
is to call forth justice
and to respect.

"You make me angry; she is driving me up the wall; he is getting under my skin; it is getting me down," are all covert ways of fingering another for my own irritation, stress, impatience, or moodiness.

The hope is vain, as ill-fated as are hopes of revenge or of reforming the other's behavior. Real hope lies in owning my choices, claiming my part in our two-person problem, learning from the errors, growing from the failure, and building more genuine and just relationships in the future.

The more subtle style of snookering others into feeling responsible for one's pain seeks to play out one's anger with passive hopes. "Hurt feelings" are the perfect ploy. "I am so hurt that you would treat me that way" expresses the hope that you will accept my definition that you are the hurter and I am the hurtee.

Passive hopes of evoking guilt, eliciting shame, and motivating change work only with those who share matching hopes that we can all be responsible for each other and are easily caught by the stratagems of the injured look. False hopes of controlling others by manipulating their consciences dissipate when one feels the urgings of real hope. Hope calls us to accept the differences that both attract and repel us and to work through them until we trust each other enough to drop the clever demands.

Magical Hopes

The struggle for an identity is a battle with time. Time competence seems simple enough. The past is "was," the future is "will be," the present is "now." But the injuries of the past keep bleeding through the skin of now, the anxieties of the

False Hopes

She hurt my feelings
And she doesn't seem to
care.
If I dwell on the hurt
(I'm not pouting, just
concerned),
If I feel, look, act hurt
(I'm not resenting, I'm just
remembering),
If I drop hints that I'm upset
(I'm not sulking, I'm just hurt),
She'll come around.
She'll feel the guilt she
needs to feel.
She'll apologize and put
herself down.
(When I can see that she hurts
Then I can feel good again.)

He may hurt me again
And he seems so
unconcerned
If I withhold complete
acceptance
(I'm not suspicious, I'm just
cautious),
If I draw back from intimate
friendship
(I'm not mistrustful, I'm just
careful),
If I drop warnings that I'm
watching
(I'm not judgmental, I have a
few qualms),
He'll be more thoughtful.
He'll be on guard, always
vigilant.
He'll guarantee that nothing
will happen.
(When I can see that he is
worried too
Then I won't need to be so
anxious.)

Hope

I am unhappy,
I am brooding,
resenting,
thinking angry,
demanding,
hurtful thoughts.
My only hope
is to quit,
to drop passive demands,
to accept
our differentness
or to work through
our differences.

I am suspicious,
I am mistrusting,
I am mind-reading,
I am judging,
evaluating,
anticipating injury
in self-fulfilling
prophecies.
My only hope
is to cancel predictions,
to confess my pretentions,
and trust you now.

future materialize to trouble the present.

Magical hopes have no time boundaries, no time realities. The hope of controlling the future by living it in advance—worry—or of mastering tomorrow by stewing on it today—brooding—is possible only for one who has no boundary between now and not yet. The hope of rewriting the past, undoing what has been done, reworking what is already history is a preoccupation for those who cannot distinguish between what is here and what was there and then.

"We do not rest satisfied with the present," wrote Pascal, "we anticipate the future as too slow in coming, as if in order to hasten its course; or we recall the past, to stop its too rapid flight. So imprudent are we that we wander in times which are not ours, and do not think of the only one which belongs to us; and so idle are we that we dream of those times which are no more, and thoughtlessly overlook that which alone exists . . . . The past and present are our means; the future alone is our end. So we never live, but we hope to live; and, as we are always preparing to be happy, it is inevitable we should never be so."[5]

Timeless hopes, born in the magical thinking of the early years must be laid aside before identity becomes a firm center. To give up the hopes of controlling the uncontrollable—tomorrow, or of reforming what is already formed—yesterday, and of dealing with the tensions that are here—now, is the nature of true hope.

Hope is a present confidence, not a fantasy of controlling the future. Hope is the calm conviction of what can be, not the illusion that what will be can be warded off or what might be can be foiled. Hope is the resource to continue trusting and

False Hopes

If I brood on what might go
wrong
(It's making me so nervous),
If I worry about what might
happen
(It's getting me so upset),
*It may help in some way
to keep it from happening.*
If I live through the impending
tragedy
(It's almost more than I can
take),
If I think of everything that
could occur
(It's got me so tight I could
snap),
*It will reduce the pain, shock,
surprise
if it should (God forbid) really
come.*

Hope

When anxiety rises
I will accept what is present
(without demanding it be
other).
I will not imagine what is
possible
(without pretending it is
reality).
I will not seek to form the
    unformed
Control the uncontrollable,
Shape the unshaped.
My hope is the acceptance
of what is here, now.
My hope is the trust
of what is not yet.
My hope is the calm
to wait for the future
without living it now.

False Hopes

If I permit only optimistic
thoughts,
(Look on the brighter side)
If I allow only positive feelings
(Hope for the best)
If I dream possibility dreams
(Something good is going to
happen)
I can escape what has been
Or elude what might be
Or evade what is.

Hope

I can face both good and evil
(Life has both light and
darkness).
I can feel both fear and calm
(Life has both joy and
sadness).
I can live in the world that is
(I need not deny, distort,
remake it).
Hope stands on what has
been.
Hope accepts what may be.
Hope challenges what is!

being trustworthy in times of threat, not an optimism that all will be well.

For Exploration in the Bible
All hoping is done in three tenses: hoping past, hoping present, hoping future. One of the most powerful metaphors used in the New Testament is of Hope as anchor—embedded in past certainties, securing the present, guaranteeing the future.

Hoping in past tense is recognizing the ground in which the anchor of the soul is embedded. This is powerfully described by the author of the letter to Jewish Christians: "So in this matter, God, wishing to show beyond doubt that his plan was unchangeable, confirmed it with an oath. So that by two utterly immutable things, the word of God and the oath of God, who cannot lie, we who are refugees from this dying world might have a source of strength, and might grasp the hope that he holds out to us. This hope we hold as the utterly reliable anchor for our souls, fixed in the innermost shrine of Heaven, where Jesus has already entered on our behalf" (Heb. 6:17-20, *Phillips*).

Hope is anchored in the acts of God for, in and among God's people in all centuries past. Hope sets its anchor in the rock bottom of what God has done in all history of humanity. From Abraham who "when hope was dead within him, went on hoping in faith" (Rom. 4:18, *Phillips*) to Christ, who is the ground of our hopes.

Hoping in the present tense is recognizing the absolute trustworthiness of God's caring for us now. The God who has given an unquestionable word, who holds out a hope to us which is beyond all contradiction.

Hoping in the future tense is claiming the

promise of the time to come, of the kingdom of God which is now and which is coming.

Such hope, rooted in what has happened, empowered by what is, excited by what will be, is a living source of strength in life.

This hope in all three tenses becomes most visible to us in our expression of and experience of prayer. Henri Nouwen describes the interaction of hoping and praying beautifully in this meditation.

Every prayer
is an expression of hope.
One who expects nothing from the future
Cannot pray.
For the prayer of hope,
it is essential that there are
no guarantees asked,
no conditions posed,
and no proofs demanded,
only that you expect everything
from the other without binding in any way.
Hope is based on the premise
that the other gives only what is good.
Hope includes an openness
by which you wait for the other
to make the loving promise come true,
even though you never know
when or where or how this might happen.
Perhaps in the long run
there is no finer image for the prayer of hope
than the relation of a child toward the mother.
All day long the child asks for things
but the love for the mother does not depend
on her fulfilling these wishes.

The child knows that the mother will do
only what is good,
and in spite of occasional fits and a few
short-lived tantrums,
if he doesn't get his way, he continues to be
convinced
that, in the end, mother does only what she
knows is best for him.[6]

Notes

1. Erik Erikson, *Insight and Responsibility* (New York: W.W. Norton & Co., Inc., 1964), p. 115.
2. Eric Fromm, *The Revolution of Hope* (New York: Harper & Row Publishers, Inc., 1968), p. 13.
3. Erikson, *Insight*, p. 117.
4. Ibid., p. 118.
5. Blaise Pascal, *Pensees*, trans. W.F. Trotter (New York: E.P. Dutton, Everyman Books, 1943), pp. 49-50.
6. Henri Nouwen, *With Open Hands* (Notre Dame, IN: Ave Maria Press, 1976), p. 82.

CHAPTER THREE

HOPES CHANGE—
HOPES MATURE
Hopes Changing, Maturing,
Unfolding in Marriage

To
travel
hopefully
is
a
better
thing
than
to
arrive.

—Robert Louis Stevenson

Hopes change.

Hopes stay the same.

True hopes change as the person grows, matures, moves through the inevitable cycle of life experiences.

False hopes tend to stay monotonously similar. Rooted as they are in our fears, our immaturity, our hidden expectations, they can remain constant, buried away within.

True hopes alter as years pass because the needs change, the tasks are different, the ways of reaching them are different in each age or stage.

False hopes shape lives, marriages, families with a stereotyped regularity and tenacity.

True hopes can set relationships growing, unfolding as people are discovering themselves and each other.

We shall examine these as they create healthy marriage, although we will discover that they exist in counterpoint with the false hopes that bedevil relationships.

False hopes, rooted so deeply, are hardy, resilient, springing back to life in times of stress. Cat-like, they possess many lives, and their end comes only when one realizes that enough is enough, that I have hoped against hope too long, that I am fed up with the fond hopes that tantalize and frustrate.

It is our hopes that bedevil early marriage. The hope of finding the perfect partner, of achieving the perfect marriage, of basking in total acceptance, of thrilling to unbroken romance, of growing together without pain or conflict, of being understood instantly and completely, of having needs met without needing to ask. Each couple's list, though different, is embarrassingly long.

Growth in covenanting a fulfilling marriage takes place in direct relationship to these hopes' demise.

The two-way transference of interlocking hopes can generally sustain a relationship up to seven years. By the tenth year it is threadbare unless the couple's ability to deny differences and avoid conflict is almost complete. As the hopes wane, a partner will say, "The marriage is so empty, hollow, I don't know if he/she cares for me anymore, maybe there's no point in going on." As the hopes die, there is grieving, sadness, not unlike the grief work surrounding the death of a much-loved friend.

Then hopes revive in the urge to divorce. "Why stay together if this is all there is? Why be connected if it is so lifeless and empty?" (The hope rises again that there is someone out there, some place where the old hopes can be fulfilled.)

When the grief work is done, the false hopes interred, the new hopes slowly rising, a marriage takes on a new life. One realizes that the reasons for one's marriage in the first place were 90 percent humbug, but the other 10 percent is not only terribly important, it is basis on which a lasting fulfilling marriage is built.

Only when a couple can say "enough is enough" to the old hopes and begin negotiating the new hopes does relationship deepen beyond the surface repetition of the old conflict patterns of the family of origin, the superficial exchange of expectations brought to the marriage. Hopes come to an end when a couple recognizes that the marriage is over on the original terms each assumed, that separation and divorce are possible now, that only when they can face leaving can they embrace staying. Then hope breaks through.

Someday My Prince Will Come

Hopes well up as courtship captivates the young person emerging from adolescence. The need for understanding, acceptance, security, meaning, identity, and intimacy become focused in the search for a person who will offer all these and, hopefully, more. The prince will come, these hopes promise, the fantasies will become reality, the dreams will come true.

If any of these wishes or longings were put into explicit words they would be denied or turned into a jest. Yet they operate on the lower layers of awareness as images of our desires, or pictures of our deepest hopes. Reality and fantasy blend into each other, each enriching, each confusing the other.

In romantic love, we are not ourselves. "I'm not sure why I say, do, act as I do," people often say, "I just can't help it." It can be described as person-addiction, as an obsession with another, or perhaps most accurately as possession. The feeling of being possessed by a totally loving person and the need to possess that person in exclusive passion is a central element of romantic loving. These are wonderful fantasies, tender and sweet, and they offer the warm reassurance of safety and security as we venture into human closeness.

Fantasy-making, that eternal process of hoping persons, is both a blessing and a curse. As blessing, it excites deep feelings for another, invests thinking time in the relationship, expands and extends the possibilities envisioned. As a curse, fantasy making can be an escape from disappointing circumstances by pretending they are otherwise, or a relief from discouragement by helping persons live with inequities or defeats. As a coercive process, fantasy can impose expectations on another which cannot be achieved.

Fantasies, like fabrics, are woven from hopes. They link the needs that press from the past with the dreams that draw us into the future.

The longing to be totally, completely understood by another reaches a high point of poignancy in teenage years, and unsatisfied, empowers the romantic spirit.

The yearning for someone to know one truly, someone who can sense what is needed with no telling required, becomes intensely attractive during youth when communicating one's thoughts, feelings, and values can be painful. This makes the hope of someone who knows my mind so desirable.

The dream of finding someone who accepts me just as I am, with no reservations, who will always be there for me no matter what may happen, calls out a dream of security that touches one at any age.

The hunger for someone who can fill up a deep and disconcerting emptiness and give life meaning prepares one to melt into another person who promises such certainty.

The passion for intimacy, sexuality, and unity with another person draws persons together— although they are both fascinated and frightened by intimacy, attracted and repelled by sexuality, intrigued and terrified by the thought of unity. These conflicted feelings all excite romance and render it even more fascinating, puzzling, and irresistible.

The rich intoxication of romantic dreams can so alter the person's world that the false hopes seem the only true reality. They promise every-

The Hopes of Courtship

Someone who understands me totally, completely.

Someone who will listen to me, find me truly interesting, really hear me.

Someone who knows me, knows what I need without my needing to ask.

Someone who accepts me just as I am without reservation.

Someone who will always be there for me, no matter what happens.

Someone who will fill up my emptiness and give my life meaning.

Someone who will tell me who I am, give me a sense of identity.

Someone who will make me a woman/man by confirming my femininity/masculinity   as desirable,   acceptable, respectable.

Someone who will offer intimacy (although I'm afraid of it), sexuality (although I'm confused about it), fidelity (although I'm both wanting and fearing being owned).

Some way to pretend that none of the above is true since we are both adults, both mature, both beyond such needs.

Remember . . . ?

Deep inside, there's a part of me that never feels understood.

Deep within, there's a part of me that never feels truly heard.

Deep inside, there's a wish for someone to offer what I need even before I ask.

Deep within, there's a longing to be loved just as I am . . .

Deep inside, there's a need for security.

Deep within, there's an empty yearning . . .

Deep inside, I wonder who I really am, and why I'm here.

Deep within, I need someone to tell me I'm really a woman/man.

Deep inside, I want (and fear) to be touched, to be loved, to be held, to belong.

But I wouldn't admit any of the above, I can't put it in words, wouldn't if I could.

thing one could wish, and hint of even more. So they prepare the lover to fuse with the other in the intense bonding of early marriage. This is an indispensable stage of the loving relationship. If there is one time when it is desirable for two persons to lose themselves in each other, to flow together as one, it is in the first stage of their developing relationship. This allows the couple to bond in a vital connection that makes space for the other and creates a joint space they will share in the more mature phases to follow.

Gradually, as persons and relationships mature, the exaggerations of inflated hopes shrink back toward the just proportionality of true hopes. The irresponsible demands that are buried in these early dreams are reconsidered and cancelled or redefined and corrected. As the true hopes emerge, the persons move toward greater mutuality, more just reciprocity, more satisfying solutions to differences, more freedom to be intimate without anxiety.

As these new hopes emerge, the mystical quality of romantic feelings turns toward a more durable and resilient affection blended with a fascination for what is actually present in the other.

"Ah Sweet Mystery of Life At Last I've Found You."

As marriage approaches, a new series of hopes emerge, triggered by the discovery of someone who is clearly "the perfect person for me." Romantic expectations rising naturally from the inner self now focus on the beloved. These expectations are a composite of unmet needs from childhood about to be met, incomplete dreams of youth about to be completed, the unsatisfied hungers of young

True Hopes of Romance

To understand another fully
as I wish to be understood.

To hear another truly
as I wish to be heard.

To know another as that person
discloses the self to be known.

To accept another deeply
as I wish to be accepted.

To be present for another
as I long for another's presence.

To accept both aloneness and togetherness,
both our separateness and our union.

To embrace and be embraced
without violating another's freedom and dignity.

To affirm another's identity without control.
To assert my own identity without dependence.

adulthood about to be fulfilled. These unverbalized expectations, if put in words, are frequently these:

"We fit each other, we are right for each other, we will never again ask 'Is this the right person for me?'" (Later we will discover that we are both right for each other and wrong for each other and it's alright to be both.)

"We will be completely fulfilled by our life together. I will never wish to be single again." (Later we will admit that there are fulfilling moments, and frustrating moments and that's OK.)

"We will be so absorbed in the happiness of our love that the romance will go on and on. I will always be surprised by the mystery the other is to me." (Sooner rather than later we will come to accept the experience of being both in romance and out of romance with the other and realize that it's quite alright.)

"Our love will be so great we will never be angry at each other; there will be no conflict, we will never regret our marriage." (The sooner the better we learn that conflict between us is not only normal and natural, it is necessary to stimulate each other's and our joint growth.)

"We will be able to provide what the other has needed all his or her life. I can be the loving father she didn't have, or the nourishing mother s/he has been searching for since childhood." (Finally we will come to realize that others must internalize their own parenting functions, to become their own mother or father, and it's alright to refuse "needs" in order to negotiate "wants.")

These hopes, though often denied during the early years of marriage, can be clearly seen in hindsight from the vantage point of mid life.

Hopes at Marriage

Remember the Hopes . . .

This is the perfect person for me (I hope).	the one
We fit each other.	for
(I will never ask, "Is this the right person?")	me
This will be the perfect marriage (I hope).	a place
We will be happy together.	for
(I will never wish to be single again.)	me
This will be an unbroken romance (I hope).	a dream
The mystery will not end.	for
(I will always find something new.)	me
This will be a smooth relationship (I hope).	a peace
There will be no pain or conflict.	for
(I will never think of leaving.)	me
There will be no failure (I hope).	a security
We will never regret our marriage.	for
(I will always be grateful.)	me
This person will fulfill all my dreams (I hope).	a parent
What was unfinished from my childhood will be completed.	for
(I will find the parent I've lost.)	me
This will create a family where I can begin again (I hope).	a justice
At last I can start again in a new, more just family.	for
(We will create a new world.)	me

Beneath the beliefs about equal relationships and mutual regard, which are the conscious goals and dreams of early marriage, lie the hopes which direct the relationship without our awareness. As the hopes mature the immaturity is increasingly recalled and reconsidered.

The hopes of a perfect partner, a flawless marriage, and an endless romance are a normal expression of early marriage bonding. If love is defined as "when another's safety, security and satisfaction is as important to me as my own," then this bonding provides a necessary time when the other becomes all-important, enabling the self to make space for a second person. The hope of finding the one for me, a place in love for me, a dream for me, a peace and security for me, a new justice for me, even a new parent for me, now bridges into the joint feelings of love. Exaggerated as the hopes may be, they serve to connect persons deeply so that maturing hopes can connect them more proportionately.

Fantasies of perfection are common in most new love, but perfectionism as a long-term style of demanding can affect some personalities lifelong.

For the perfectionist, the hopes of a perfect partner, perfect marriage, perfect relationship continue to grow as the years pass. The perfectionistic person often has great trouble finding an acceptable partner, since no one matches the demanded ideal. Once a person is found, the ideal may be loved more than the real.

"The perfectionistic person often looks upon marriage as another achievement. Once married, he does not know how to enjoy it, or she continues her old perfectionistic attitudes, demanding perfect order. He becomes anxious if the house is not in order at all times, with eggs done to a split-second three minutes, toast to a certain shade of tan, shirts starched a certain way, and perfect children from his perfect wife. His anxiety leads him to demand these things because anything less than what he considers 'perfect' arouses his childhood patterns of self-belittlement. Many a husband silently accepts his perfectionistic wife's demands that he not wear shoes in the living room because she fears marks on her perfect rugs, endures her corrections of his speech, and indeed never feels comfortable himself."[1]

The hopes that empower perfectionism are complex. There may be the hope of finally earning affection and approval. Or there may be the hope of proving oneself acceptable to an inner tyrant. Or there may be the hope of at last matching an internalized ideal, no matter how exaggerated or impossible. Or there may be the hope of at last disproving a hidden sense of inferiority. Most frequently it is a combination of all of the above, operating on both conscious and unconscious levels.

The hopes must be surfaced, and "the courage of imperfection" affirmed as the only true human wisdom. Such courage confronts one's inner judge by claiming vulnerability in the face of its demands. The freedom from tyrannical "shoulds and oughts" is won bit by bit, by letting go and letting be.

"Love Is More Lovely the Second Time Around"

Every person or couple should experience at least three marriages. To spend one's whole life in one marriage is to choose to remain immature and to refuse growth.

The three marriages, for maximum growth, should be with the same partner. Effective marriage is a serial polygamy with the same person. The renegotiation, recovenanting, rediscovery of the other occurs at, at least, two crucial passages, although for many of us there are three or four such turning points when the marriage is renewed, even revolutionized.

Marriage is the natural healing and growth process in western culture. It is the context that brings out the weaknesses and the strengths in each person and in the relationship. It provides an occasion for growth in small increments or in larger steps of breakthrough, throughout the whole life cycle.

Love is more lovely the second, the third, even the fourth time around. The maturing of loving relationship allows greater freedom for each, greater security for both; greater respect for the person, greater intimacy in the relationship. Such maturing of love takes place with couples who move through the three marriages with the same partners; it also occurs with persons who divorce and begin again with second partners, although for these the plot becomes more complex since the original actors never fully leave the stage. First partners, though silent partners in a reconstituted family, continue their influence in both positive and negative ways whether those involved recognize it or not.

"Marriage is an irrevocable trust for the lifetime of the participants," says John Warkentin, a leading marital theorist. "The income from it may be withdrawn but the principle always remains." One invests his or her emotional capital in the first marriage, and it cannot be gotten back. One may

By letting go,
it all gets done;
The world is won
by those who let it go!
But when you try and try,
the world is then
beyond the winning.

—Lao Tzu[2]

By letting be
I become free to grow.
I change and mature
not when I am trying
to be different than I am,
but when I am accepting
who, what, where I am.

By letting go and letting be
we become free to grow together.
A marriage matures
not when we are trying to perfect it,
but when we are accepting each other
for who and what we are
and where we each stand.

invest the interest from this capital in a second marriage, but the capital cannot be recovered. "When two persons are married emotionally, they have irrevocably committed feelings that they cannot withdraw again and place with another."[3]

The most effective journey toward maturity is to experience one marriage after another with the same partner. Each marital state has a contribution to make. Each has its own demands, expectations and hopes. The three basic marriages and the hopes that direct them can be called oneness, twoness, and threeness.

Marriage One: Oneness

In the first months of marriage, the two fuse into one. The boundaries go down, personalities flow into each other so that an emotional glob occurs. The two fuse all the way to their core selves. For those with little core, there is little left except the wonderful joint emotional blob of the two now blended into each other.[4]

Emotionally, this is experienced as a deep sense that "we are we," and the we-ness obliterates the I-ness which was gained in identity formation, and blinds us to the distinct you-ness that was seen in courtship and engagement.

Beneath the visible surface differences of the two persons entering early marriage, lie deep strata of hopes for oneness, sameness, and idealness.

The hope of oneness is felt as an impulse to think alike, feel alike, choose alike, become more alike. The boundaries experienced in becoming a single person in young adulthood now become blurred or even destroyed.

The hope of sameness is not just that we be

MARRIAGE ONE	MARRIAGE TWO	MARRIAGE THREE
Oneness "We are we"	*Twoness* "I am I and you are you"	*Threeness* "I am I and you are you and we are we"
Fusion of two melding into one (But which one?)	Separation of two struggling for identity— I will be I, you may be you	Reunion of two with separate selves and shared covenant
Romantic illusions— We are the Dream. (Your dream? or mine?)	Loss of illusions— Where have the flowers gone? (Who am I, who are you?)	Reality of intimacy— I can love you as you. (Why did it take so long to find each other?)
YEARS ONE TO SEVEN	**YEARS EIGHT TO FIFTEEN**	**YEARS FIFTEEN TO FIFTY**
Complementary relationships: dominant-submissive nourisher-nourished dependent-independent fixed roles each defined by relationship to the other. *Conflict is suppressed.*	Symmetrical Relationships: Two dependent persons struggling for equal freedom and acting independent in reactive roles. *Conflict is cyclical.*	Parallel Relationships: Two equally mature persons each claiming freedom to be a whole self while covenanting mutuality. *Conflict is negotiated.*

similar in our oneness, but that "things will always be like this, always stay the same." The hope of a secure permanence is experienced as a wish for our love to never change, for the present affection and passion to go on as it is, forever. Later, the hope of permanence accepts great change in the terms of the relationship, but without losing its constancy.

The hope of idealness looks for perfection in the other, pretends perfection in the self, and demands that we both join in fulfilling the dream each thinks we share. Later we will come to see how different our dreams really are, but when "we are we" in the sweet fusion of a new relationship, each assumes that love unites our deepest yearnings.

In the "oneness marriage" two persons fuse in order to bond with each other. This is a necessary giving up of a large part of the self to make a full connection with another person. The more firm the sense of single identity in each person, the more core self remains in this conjoint existence period; the less identity, the less one or both have left. In the oneness of romance we discover the positive sides of ourselves, of which we are unaware, in the other. All the warm and beautiful hopes, longings, dreams, and tender feelings deep in the unknown depths of ourselves are projected onto the other. The feelings that are buried beneath this process are expressed; they are "You are my hopes, my dream, my happiness, my reason for living." Later in the transition into Marriage Two the negative parts of the self will be projected on the other person, and each will see the undesirable aspects of their own personality magnified in the other person, and feel a hatred for the

False Hopes of Marriage

Every marriage is actually three sequential marriages.

MARRIAGE ONE: ONENESS

"We are we."

The hope of oneness: we will be one and the same, think alike, feel alike, choose alike, we've got each other.

The hope of permanence: what we have will never change, things will go on as they are, forever.

The hope of perfection is self and other, We will each fulfill the dream we share.

MARRIAGE TWO: TWONESS

"I am I—you are you."

The hope of returning to the sweet fusion of early marriage, to pretend nothing is changing.

The hope of remaking the other to match the dream, the dream that is fading as we admit our differences.

The hope of restoring the old romance of recovering the illusions, the excitement, the mystery.

MARRIAGE THREE: THREENESS

"I am I—you are you—we are we."

The hope of reaching a stable static period when all our changes are past.

The hope of finally having it all together so we can relax for the long haul.

The hope that we can maintain youthfulness, avoid aging, escape mortality, evade loneliness.

other, which is really self-hate. When each can discover his or her own centered identity, and be at peace with the self, the war with the other subsides. When the conflict within is resigned, the conflict between can be resolved.

As two people form a marriage, they are directed by the hope that two mature, capable, self-reliant persons can share a life made rich by each person's gifts and wisdom. The hope is that two independent identities can form an interdependent relationship which stimulates the health and growth of both.

But beneath these healthy hopes lie another series of hidden hopes of dependency. There are moments in our relationships when it is proper and necessary to be dependent, but when our temporary dependencies become fixed and permanently built into our interpersonal arrangements, then we come to expect others to take responsibility for us, or conversely, to let us take responsibility for them (which is another way of taking care of ourselves by taking care of others). So we create conspiracies rather than relationships, a collusion rather than a marriage.

Some of these collusions are:

1. I'll be the parent—you be the child.
2. I'll be the worker—you be the player.
3. I'll be responsible—you can be irresponsible.
4. I'll be the healthy one—you be the sick one.
5. I'll be the leader—you be the follower.
6. I'll be the tyrant—you be the victim.
7. I'll be the taker—you be the giver.
8. I'll be right—you always be wrong.
9. I'll be the protector—you be the protected.
10. I'll be friendly—you be distant.[5]

Any couple can draw on at least two or three of these conspiracies when these false hopes of avoiding self-responsibility shape their relationship unconsciously. These illusions of one–up–one–down complementarity are learned in our families of origin, are exaggerated by our own immaturities, and become fixed in our early attempts to work out how we will fit together. Our joint illusions become collusions.

In Marriage One, the illusions that connect the lovers are greater than the reality, although both believe that they are reality. The illusions unite the two, providing the needed connections until the sinews of more authentic love can develop. When the relationship is knit together by the real rather than the ideal, the two find each other in greater authenticity. Illusions must fade for intimacy to begin, it cannot grow without reality. Two shadows can converge, but not touch.

But in early marriage, the relationship is so fragile that the illusions are necessary to protect and insulate it. When the two begin to feel somewhat secure, they transmit a new signal to each other. "It's safe now, all clear, we can get down to real issues, we can let the romance pass."

"In the midst of the marital struggle, the honeymoon dream vanishes, and the despair over the old relationship comes up for re-examination. Suddenly each spouse turns the eyes away from the partner, and looks inwardly and asks, 'What am I doing to my partner? What is wrong with me? What am I misunderstanding? What must I do to rescue this marriage?' If honestly asked, the answers are not far behind: 'I really married my wife because of her difference. It is not my job to make her over, but rather to discover and to value

Marriage One
"Oneness Is Everything"

False Hopes	True Hopes
We can become one. Question: but which one?	We can be united Yet separate persons.
We can stay the same. Question: but why are we bored?	We can be together lifelong, Yet changing, growing, surprising.
We can live the dream. Question: but whose dream?	We can give up our dreams Since loving a real person is better.

that difference. But before I can do that I must accept my difference and I really need her to help me discover my uniqueness.'"[6]

The element in a couple's relationship that initiates this change and sustains them through the struggle is hope, a very specific kind of hope that rises from the intensity of the commitment between them. It is the hope so powerful that it is a guarantee that we will stay together to work through any problem. Without this hope, couples tend only to touch this need for change, and rebound back into the old oneness.

Marriage Two: Twoness

As the "we are we" of initial fusion begins its transformation, the "I am I AND you are you" of the second marriage emerges. As each person enters the third decade of life, responsibility for oneself becomes internalized. In marriage, this sense of self-responsibility and accountability with others appears in the recovery of a sense of identity that clarifies one's position in the most intimate relationship of one's life.

Affirming that I am I, separate and distinct from the you that is you, is a painful, a threatening, a tearing and rending experience. The old attachment, woven richly with illusions, must be torn gently or at times roughly so that new connections of a more reverent reality may be covenanted.

As the twoness evolves, the heart is torn by forces pulling in opposite directions; false hopes draw one back toward the remembered closeness of the first fusion, true hopes tug one outward toward a new relationship.

The hope of going back to the first romantic love invites many couples to silently conspire to

Marriage Two
"Twoness Is Necessary"

False Hopes	True Hopes
We can go back to the old romance. Question: but how do we close our eyes?	If I let go of the romance I can discover a rich respect.
We can slip back into the old fusion. Question: but can I hide how I've changed?	If I can be truly I Then we can be fully we.
I can remake the other into my dream. Question: but why isn't it your dream too?	If I can cancel the illusions I can discover a beautiful reality.

deny the differences that are becoming clear and to settle for a facade of togetherness. The hope of recovering or pretending the sweet fusion of early marriage can thwart the healthful growth into twoness by a return to oneness.

The hope of turning time back, like all false hopes, requires a second hope to support it—the hope of remaking the other to match the old dreams which are now fading as we are forced to face our differences. People cannot be changed from without in any lasting ways. Changes that endure are made slowly, and from within. But the illusory hopes of remaking another to match one's prescriptions are as pretentious as they are powerless.

The hope of restoring the old romance, of recovering the excitement, of regaining the mystery, lies behind the strategies of reoccupying the past. These hopes must die before hope can be released to link us together with enduring faith here in this relationship, now in this moment.

As this change occurs, the illusions of romance turn to the reality of respect, a respect rich in affection and commitment, yet secure in its recognition of the other as distinctly different, separate, an autonomous self.

As persons struggle to reclaim their separate identities, the recovery of twoness seems the death of the relationship. As false hopes die, fear springs up, the fear that the loving relationship will be lost, that nothing will remain once the old oneness has evaporated. For some, the fear is so overwhelming that they flee the changing relationship to quickly consummate another. People in such transitions can be candidates for an affair. As the old fusion is waning, the one person may look for another equally absorbing attachment. The affair may be sexual, vocational, chemical or even spiritual. It may be with money, with athletics, with the arts; it may be a garden, a sailboat, the stock market, or any other consuming passion. One may look for a person who invites a return to all-embracing oneness, or for a vocation that is totally consuming, or a chemical dependency that takes complete control, or a spiritual addiction that becomes obsessive. Such an affair is the most common escape from facing the anxiety aroused by the separation of the first "we-ness" into the distinct identities of "I am I AND you are you." Only when this is becoming firm and clear does the third marriage begin.

Marriage Three: Threeness

In mature marriage, there are three separate yet interlocking entities. I, you, and we. "I am I AND you are you AND we are we." As each becomes his and her self, the relationship becomes more clearly visible to both. They can see it, speak of it, negotiate it, celebrate it, deal with it, almost as if it were a third person in each of their lives. The "we are we" is no longer a combination of each person's hopes fused into a largely unconscious oneness. The relationship is now a consciously covenanted union of two whole persons who value self and other equally, and prize their common life together as an infinitely precious entity to be guarded, nourished, protected, and celebrated. This new "we are we" now guarantees both intimacy and identity, both autonomy and solidarity, both togetherness and separateness.

In a mature marriage, the relationship has a life of its own, each nurtures and cares for, as well

For marriage. I use a bicycle analogy.
If a couple is differentiated,
They're both riding bicycles
down a country road
and they're side by side.
Each is caring enough to regulate their speed.
In tandem, they ride separately together.
Sometimes, one can go faster than the other
but it's always with caring
always noticing how the other is coming along
so that one doesn't get too far ahead,
or one doesn't lag too far behind.
Each uses their own power
to keep their own bike going.

In the first stage of marriage
one rides the handle bars
while one supplies the power.
In the beginning it's easier
to just go along for the ride
so the dependent partner rides
and dominant partner pedals.

In the second stage of marriage
the rider will kick the pedaler off
so they can change direction,
go faster or slower
but at this time they are still competing
for the same bike,
and fighting over who supplies the power
and who is determining the direction.
So separate bikes become important
to enable them to ride together.

In the third stage,
they may be ready for a bicycle-built-for-two.
Then they both can supply equal power
or one can rest a while without being left behind.[7]

as trusts and respects, the integrity of this covenant that connects and protects them both.
Mature love is a creative tension at the boundary
point of separateness and togetherness. It insures
togetherness while guaranteeing separateness.
Love links union and separation: it promises the
warmth of closeness while pledging the requisite
distance. The two are bound together and freed to
be apart.

The German poet Rainer Maria Rilke pictures
this in his words of prophecy of the movement
from the traditional roles of the Victorian age to
the increased mutuality of the twentieth century.

> Once the realization is accepted
> That even between the closest human
> beings
> Infinite distances continue to exist.
> A wonderful living side by side can grow up,
> If they succeed in loving the distance
> between them
> Which makes it possible for each to see the
> other
> Whole and against a wide sky.[8]

The love of the bonding-space/breathing-space
between is as important as the love of the other; all
three points in the relationship must be foci of
their love, all three must be guarded and prized
equally.

False hopes accompany us unto the third marriage and shape this relationship as well.

The hope that we have arrived at a point of
calm, a place of mature safety, a position that is
beyond conflict can create a new kind of denial,
not unlike the very first. This is marked by a kind

Marriage Three
"Threeness Is We-ness"

False Hopes

We have arrived at a point
of calm.
A place of mature safety,
A position that is beyond
conflict.
We've finally got it all
together.
Question: so why do we still
have problems?

We have reached a static
stable period.
Our major developmental
changes are over.
If we are normal, there will
be little change.
Question: so why do we
keep changing?

We have an unlimited time
to live and grow.
We can stop time and stay
young,
We will be safe indefinitely.
Death cannot happen to me
or my partner.

True Hopes

We will have moments of
calm and conflict,
times of tranquility and
tension.
We will work it out together
although we will never have
it all together.

We will grow,
We will change,
We will have different styles,
different rates, different
goals.
We will work to grow
together.

We will be alive
all the days of our lives.
We will face our mortality,
accept our humanness,
share our sadness or grief.

of stagnation within the person and a boredom between them. As this marital truce of coexistence fades, deeper hopes appear—hopes of living in the ongoing drama of give and take, of joining and separating, of testing each other's strength, and sharing each other's weakness. The true hope that is born is a hope of the other's constant presence, consistent caring, and inevitable honesty and openness about his or her perspective on the relationship and on the other person.

Even in mature marriage we cannot hope that we are now finally committed in unaltering permanence. Marriage is a renewable, renegotiable contract all life long, and the clearer the understanding that we will be together lifelong, the greater the freedom to renegotiate and renew the terms of life arrangements.

The hope of a static, stable calm in mid and later marriage still prevails. "As long as marriage is seen as a static arrangement between two unchanging people, any substantial change in either of those people must initially be perceived as a violation of the contract. It sets off guilt in one partner and developmental envy in the other, because it's not 'supposed to happen.' Supposedly, we're to be defined by our partner's need for security and to move only when the other is ready or with his/her agreement. Such a contract makes us other-defined; it distances us from self-directing impulses and adds an imprisoned quality to our life."[10]

The true hopes of growth welcome movement by either partner. He or she is not threatened by the lover's change. The sense of surprise and resistance within the self is used as a signal that something important is taking place in the mar-

A good relationship
Has a pattern like a dance
And is built on some
Of the same rules.

The partners do not need to hold on tightly,
Because they move confidently
In the same pattern,
Intricate but gay and swift and free,
Like a country dance of Mozart's.

There is no place here
For the possessive clutch,
The clinging arm, the heavy hand;
Only the barest touch in passing.

Now arm in arm,
Now face to face,
Now back to back—
It does not matter which.
Because they know they are partners
Moving to the same rhythm,
Creating a pattern together,
And being invisibly nourished by it.[9]

—Anne Morrow Lindbergh

riage. However, there are five steps of resistance to change that are as normal as a plant turning to the sun. When a partner alters a basic pattern of our life together or breaks one of the "rules" we have either assumed or agreed on, there are six inevitable steps in the response: (1) Don't change, (2) change back, (3) threat, (4) grudging respect, (5) the other pulls up in initiative to change, (6) then the person will say, "That's what I tried to tell you all along, what took you so long?"[11] The more aware we are of this normal pattern of resistance, the more we can smile and accept the other's movement as an invitation to grow. So we move from marriage to marriage, we divorce old arrangements but not the person. Living through the rhythms of one's own maturing growth while testing these against the push and pull of someone you love (who is moving through a parallel journey of change) creates a dynamic and richly meaningful relationship.

A third cluster of hopes, both false and true, center in our attitudes toward life and death, present and future, fear and loss.

The hopes that we have an unlimited time to live and grow, that we will go on forever are false. The time myth is a way of avoiding the reality of not only the future but of the present. If I have no clear concept of the future, I will be less aware of the preciousness of the now. If I cannot face what will be, I will avoid what is threatening among the things that are.

The hopes that we can stop and stay young are false. To refuse to live in each decade of your life is to refuse to live. Those who pretend that they are still in their twenties, thirties, or forties when they are one or more decades beyond are missing the

I am I
You are you
But if I am I
because you are you,
then I am not I.
And if you are you
because I am I
then you are not you.
So I shall be I
And you must be you.

—Rabbi Mendel of Kiosk

I will prize my I-ness
I will honor your you-ness.
If my I-ness is lost in your you-ness,
Or your you-ness in my I-ness,
Our we-ness is impoverished.

privilege of living in that actual time period. To miss one's fifties, sixties, seventies is to miss out on a rich part of one's life cycle. The delight of marriage is to mesh the rhythms of two lives into a joint dance toward maturity.

The hopes that we will be safe indefinitely, that death cannot happen to me or to my partner, that our lives will be uninterrupted by one of us facing major illness or death are vain hopes. The more mature a person is, the clearer the concept of the future, the sharper is the reality of death. I, you, we shall die. As the illusions about death die, the realities of living and dying can be woven together to give each moment depth. Not that one dwells on death, but knowing how short life is, how precious this moment, how few the opportunities to be truly present with each other, one savors each experience with a sense of reverence, gratitude and awe.

The Central Hopes of Intimacy

The central hopes of a life shared with another human being would be ranked differently by any person, yet the basic cluster is similar for us all. The ten most important elements in marriage are placed in order of preference as selected by partners in marriages described as satisfyingly happy. Within these elements of love, laughter, communication, involvement, friendships, integrity, tolerance, adaptability, sexual intimacy, and sharing are the central hopes of loving relationship.

As these hopes are recognized and shared with the other, a genuine intimacy is mellowing and becoming more mutually satisfying. As the hopes are felt and followed in parallel trust the two no longer cling to each other in neediness, but they

Central Hopes of Intimacy

The Most Important Elements in Marriage

Hopes of love
I hope to be prized as equally precious
even as I know both of us are equally
worthful.

Love
Prizing the other as
equally precious, feeling
caring, trust, intimacy.

Hopes of humor
I hope to laugh often, laugh freely, laugh
happily in the shared joy, mirth, celebration.

Laughter
Delighting in the humor of
a situation, laughing freely.

Hopes of understanding
I hope to be heard for who I truly am even
as I want to hear you as you are.

Conversation
Listening and speaking
with both thoughts and
feelings, information and
emotion.

Hopes of meaning
I hope to share a life purpose and project
in a joint commitment to goals beyond
ourselves.

Involvement
Committing ourselves to a
sense of purpose outside
ourselves and our joint
relationship.

Hopes of friendship
I hope to delight in companionship with you
and to free us both to enjoy our own
friends.

Friendships
Enjoying both individual
and joint friends, alone
and together.

Hopes of integrity
I hope to be congruent within myself, and
consistently trustworthy in relationships.

Integrity
Being a person who is
trustworthy, dependable,
and principled.

Hopes of acceptance
I hope to accept you as you are and to be
accepted for who and what I am.

Tolerance
Accepting the other's
weaknesses, quirks,
moods.

Hopes of flexibility
I hope to bend, change, adapt, grow, and
to experience your flexibility in life.

Adaptability
Accepting the other's
uniqueness, differences;
adjusting in give and take.

Hopes of sexuality
I hope to be free to celebrate embodiment
and invite you to be fully, bodily alive.

Sex
Sharing fulfillment in
mutual intimacy and
celebration of the body.

Hopes of co-working
I hope for meaning in our working and
creating, And the deepest joy will be in
serving together.

Sharing
Sharing jobs, projects,
roles, thoughts,
information, etc.[12]

brush tenderly in the respect that comes from a shared history, a tested resiliency, a confidence that comes from years of working through both the trivial and the crucial issues.

In letting the false hopes come to awareness, and die, we set free the hope within.

For Exploration of the Bible

Hope is rooted in faith and empowered by love.

Listen to Saint Paul's words on this network of strength that unites faith, hope and love.

"Love knows no limit to its endurance,
no end to its trust, no fading of its hope;
it can outlast anything. It is, in fact,
the one thing that still stands
when all else has fallen . . . . In this
life we have three great lasting qualities—
faith, hope and love.
But the greatest of these is love" (1 Cor. 13:7-8,13, *Phillips*).

To sense how deep is the rooting of faith and love in the soil of hope, examine the following diagramming of their interdependence.

Love knows no limit to its endurance.
(Enduring love is hopeful, faithful love.)
Love knows no end to its trust.
(Trusting love is hopeful, faithful love.)
Love knows no fading of its hope.
(Hopeful love can outlast anything.)
Love still stands when all else has fallen.
(Faithful love is eternal.)

The conjunction of faith, hope and love shapes all effective human relationships. Hope provides the basis for being, love the content, and faith the enduring meaning.

In the covenant of marriage, hope makes the covenant possible, love gives it the content of equal regard, and faith provides the enduring constancy and fidelity.

"The greatest of these is love," Saint Paul concludes, but he might have said, "The first of these is hope."

Notes
1. Hugh Missildine, *Your Inner Child of the Past* (New York: Simon & Schuster, Inc., 1963), p. 91.
2. Lao Tzu, *The Way of Life* (New York: Mentor Books, 1955), p. 101.
3. John Warkentin, "Family Systems Theory," *Family Dynamics* (Palo Alto, CA: Science and Behavior, 1969), p. 12.
4. Murray Bowen, *Family Therapy in Clinical Practice* (New York: Aronson, Jason, Inc., 1978), p. 12.
5. Roger Gould, *Transformations* (New York: Simon & Schuster, Inc., 1978), p. 279.
6. Abraham Schmitt, "Conflict and Ecstacy—Model for Maturing Marriage," unpublished paper.
7. Barbara Lynch, "Couples: How They Develop and Change," *News*, Gestalt Institute of Cleveland, Fall, 1982.
8. Rainer Maria Rilke, quoted by Anne Morrow Lindbergh, *Gift from the Sea* (New York: Random House, Inc., 1955).
9. Ibid., p. 104.
10. Gould, *Transformations*, p. 279.
11. Bowen, *Family Therapy*, p. 467ff.
12. Sol Gordon, "10 Most Important Things in Marriage," *Good Housekeeping*, April 1978, pp. 58-60.

CHAPTER FOUR

TRUE HOPES— FALSE HOPES
Hopes Canceled, Hopes Created in Family Living

Hope means to keep living
amid desperation,
and to keep humming
in the darkness.
Hope is knowing
that there is love;
it is trust in tomorrow;
it is falling asleep
and waking again
when the sun rises.
In the midst of a gale at sea
it is to discover land.
In the eyes of another
it is to see that he understands you.

—Henri Nouwen[1]

To know a family, one must know its hopes.

Within each family system lies a network of hopes, hopes that are deeply prized, firmly held, and rarely expressed in words. Yet these hopes direct how they handle differences, manage stress, express feelings, offer love, and work through problems. In short, a family's hopes determine how they relate and communicate.

If every human relationship is an extension of those person's hopes, then a family is a living network of hopes, shaped by tradition, policed by sanctions from generation to generation.

The "peace-agree" family has elaborated its hopes into myths, like the myth of peace that affirms it is absolutely essential for persons to evade all tensions in relationship, or the myth of agreement that affirms it is unquestionably crucial to avoid all differences in the family. Such myths can only be sustained if the family is willing to pay the price of denial. "Differences? What differences? We really agree! Tensions? What tensions? We couldn't be happier!"

The "strictly-logical" family has embroidered its hopes into the myths of being (1) stoic without tender emotions and/or (2) rational without any subjective emotional conclusions. Such myths can only be upheld by the sacrifice of one-half of reality. We are both rational and emotive beings, both objective and subjective. Wholeness as persons and health in family living requires that we surface such myths and challenge the hopes that energize them.

The hopes, the myths, and the kinds of families that they produce are varied, and yet painfully similar. The dreams of escaping life's normal stresses and suppressing the natural human

HAPPY FAMILIES
ARE ALL ALIKE,
EACH UNHAPPY FAMILY
IS UNHAPPY IN
ITS OWN WAY.

—Tolstoy, *Anna Karenina*

The Reverse Is True

Happy families develop in a wide variety of styles, types, patterns. They offer a rich freedom and develop in an exciting variety of ways.

Unhappy families are tragically similar. It is as if they are locked into a relatively limited number of family scripts, driven by similar hopes, patterned by common myths, shaped by the same denial of reality.

impulses create a common pattern of denial. Denial families are locked into an amazingly similar set of "scripts" or "patterns" of relating to each other.

Families are formed by their hopes. Their hopes motivate, instruct, protect, direct and also distort their lives. Family hopes are the most basic expression of their core values, of what shapes their central beliefs.

Yet they are rarely put into words. The hopes emerge in the myths a family honors by the way they relate to each other. These myths are the embodiment of their most basic hopes. These myths serve several basic functions in the family— to instruct the members on how to relate to one another, to obscure the past with its troubling unfinished business, and to protect the family against outsiders by serving as smoke screens that hide embarrassing or threatening experiences—often called "family secrets."

These beliefs are truly myths because they are held as basic assumptions without being examined, trusted without being tested. They are myths because, as arbitrary beliefs, they are held as traditions from one generation to the next without reflection or discussion permitted. The basic group of hopes that form family myths are, not surprisingly, quite similar from family to family. They form a common cluster of myths that recur with a stubborn frequency. Most families in western cultures suffer from at least six out of these eight myths like a chronic condition of denial and distortion.

The Common Cluster of Hopes
There is a common cluster of hopes that rise in

human relationships—the hopes for peace, safety, security, strength, success, love. These can be true hopes that yearn for the basic values of loving and trustworthy relationship. Or these same hopes can be woven into a binding web of false expectations.[2]

The hope for peace can be turned into a dream of escaping all tensions, avoiding stress, evading anxiety.

The hope for togetherness can become a wish for no differences, no conflict, no diversity.

The hope for acceptance can grow into a demand that there be no criticism, no negatives, no confrontation.

The hope for harmony can emerge as an attempt at feeling no anger, no arousal, no hostile feelings.

The hope for love can be distorted into a need to control, manipulate, dominate.

The hope for adequacy can be expressed as a belief that tender, sad, or painful feelings must be suppressed or denied.

The hope for logic can become a demand for no subjective feelings, no emotionality, no craziness.

The hope for success can make one afraid of failure, frightened by facing any imperfections.

So the necessary hopes of effective relationships—peace, togetherness, acceptance, harmony, love, adequacy, logic, and success—can become the false hopes of homogenizing people and relationships. This hope of eliminating the normal tensions, differences, conflicts, anger, sadness, and weakness blocks personal and family health, and stifles growth. The false hopes gradually swallow up the true. Many families live by this cluster of false hopes and pass them along from

False Hopes of Families

A HOPE FOR NO TENSIONS
(If one can be sweet, surface, cheerful, then tensions can be avoided. So *niceness is necessary.*)

A HOPE FOR NO DIFFERENCES
(If one can be agreeable, compliant, adaptable, then differences can be erased. Since *differences are dangerous.*)

A HOPE FOR NO CRITICISM
(If one can communicate cautiously, with questions, cleverly with concealed or indirect messages, then criticism can be escaped. Since *comments are criticism.*)

A HOPE FOR NO ANGER
(If one can hide, suppress, deny, or defer anger, then negative feelings can be eliminated. Since *anger is attack.*)

A HOPE FOR NO WEAKNESS
(If one can hide pain, stifle tears, conceal sadness then one will appear strong and invulnerable. Since *sadness is weakness.*)

A HOPE FOR NO DISOBEDIENCE
(If one can gain another's love, they will have to be loyal, obedient, conforming to the lover's demands. Since *love is control.*)

A HOPE FOR NO CRAZINESS
(If one can keep all debate perfectly reasonable, then all feelings can be kept in their place. Since *logic is the last word.*)

A HOPE FOR NO FAILURE
(If one can strive to be completely adequate, successful, perfect, one is safe. Since *failure is final.*)

generation to generation as well-believed myths. These myths become so deeply ingrained in the family psyche that, although they may be rarely verbalized, they are constantly present and active in the family's daily functioning. Myths have power, and they gather their power from their great control of the unconscious. Once afloat in the family psyche they become an elemental force in each member's personality. Myths are learned early, learned deeply, learned all in a piece as a network of interlocking convictions that function as family rules.

The power of family myths as expressions of family hopes is best seen in life stories. The eight myths most commonly demonstrated in both healthy and troubled families, although to different degrees, will be illustrated, charted in full-page descriptions, and challenged by contrasting them with demonstrated realities in human relationships.

Myth 1: Niceness Is Necessary

"If you don't have something good to say, then you better not say anything at all," the mother used to say, not aware that what she had just said was not a good thing to say. But it was nice, and in this family, niceness was next to godliness. Cheerfulness was an absolute necessity. They were so positive that it hurt, their faces were fixed in perma-smiles, but underneath there was a lot of collected resentments. There was nothing else to do with resentments but to let them accumulate, and niceness covered them all.

Niceness has as many forms as there are anxious people. But the goal is the same—to keep relationships as surface as possible so that buried conflicts do not surface, or to keep interactions superficial so that troublesome feelings, needs, and personal issues get ignored.

"In my family, we didn't talk much. And what we did was small talk. Business. Weather. Schedule. The day's events. But no feelings, no real statements about our inner struggles, no risks, no revelations. We knew a lot about each other, but, although we were a family, we did not know each other."

Niceness invites niceness. When this is a genuine gentleness, it creates trusting relationships of intimacy and warmth. When this is the united front so typical of "good people," then the niceness insures distance and avoidance but with the best of conscious intentions. Habitual niceness inhibits the free expression of the normal negative feelings that occur simultaneously with positive feelings in all interactions. It prohibits the easy discussion and resolution of differences making it hard to initiate frank interchanges. How dare one report negative feelings to someone who is so nice? So participants are kept on guard by the fear that their relationship could not survive a hassle if one should erupt spontaneously. When anxiety does arise, the solutions sought are superficial, since the major concern is how to restore the peace, not how to resolve the differences. In nice families, conflict is inevitably over secondary issues—like fighting over who started the problem, or who's responsible for the open fight, or who can be intimidated to never do it again. The need to restore the peace, keep the peace, or even pretend there is peace is greater than the concern for resolving the real issues that lie a little further down.

If I Hope to Live with No Tension or Stress

Then cheerful tact
and sweet politeness
become the basis
of life together.
Tensions must be temperate,
frustrations forgotten,
irritations ignored,
stress is suppressed.
Each must find some way
to get what is wanted
without open request
or frank demand.
Since (above all else)—
NICENESS IS NECESSARY.
(Let's hope we can always be nice.)

Let the hope die.

A balance of genuineness and gentleness,
a wholeness of loving and leveling,
caring for others and candor with others,
invite growth, excite health and stimulate depth
in all human relationships.
Not superficial niceness,
but a deep genuineness
creates trust, builds faith, nourishes love.
Since (above all else)—
GENUINENESS ENABLES GROWTH.

Not niceness, but genuineness given in gentleness is the key to real growth, health, and human warmth. And that requires some risking, some sharing of the whole self, some vulnerability. One must hope for more than the calm of no tensions. Such hopes are false anyway. One must hope for the mutual peacemaking that helps us find each other with integrity.

Myth 2: Differences Are Dangerous

"To differ with my dad is to be considered a disobedient or rebellious kid. I'm not supposed to have any opinions except those of the management. But I do. So I keep my thoughts to myself. Nobody notices, we're all that way in our family. We don't dare differ."

In this family, as in many, "to differ is to reject." The freedom to think one's own thoughts and feel one's own feelings is limited by the quiet pressure to think as one ought and feel as one should. The personal boundaries that define where one person ends and another begins become blurred. The sacredness of each person's own voluntary choice is violated. The reverence for each person's responsibility to live authentically as a self before God and with others is lost as people play god for each other, or let others be their god or master. (One can live in fear of, reverence for, subservience to another or others without their knowing or desiring it.)

"When someone disagrees with me, I get tight in the chest, then a knot appears in my stomach. I can't handle it when someone important to me feels very differently about things that really matter. In my family, disagreement was seen as disrespect so we didn't talk about the things that could

If I Hope to Live
with No Differences

Then variations in thinking,
differences in feeling,
contrasts in perspective,
conflicts in behaving
are all seen as threat,
or viewed as betrayal,
or treated as rebellion.
Disagreement is seen as disrespect,
differing is viewed as rejecting;
so we must claim agreement,
be adaptable and compliant,
even if we have to fake it.
Since (beware)—
DIFFERENCES ARE DANGEROUS.
(Let's hope we can always agree.)

Let the hope die.

The natural variety in viewpoints,
diversity in preferences,
contrasts in perspectives,
uniqueness of persons,
are to be prized,
are to be enhanced,
are to be celebrated.
Variety and diversity
complete us, fulfill us.
Since (beware)—
DIVERSITY IS DESIRABLE.

bring out our differences. We acted as though we were identical, like, 'you've seen one Smith, you've seen them all.'"

In the healthy family, the freedom to think for one's self, to feel as one truly feels, to believe as one is choosing to believe, freely and from within, are all prized and protected. Each individual's own integrity as a thinking, feeling, choosing, believing person is respected. Understandings and agreements are negotiated and covenanted, not coerced or assumed.

The fear of difference is the root of immaturity. The assumption that the world is like me, actually an extension of me, is a normal part of early childhood, but it is dropped as the child discovers that the other is truly an "other," and that it is possible to step outside one's own perspective and view the world from another's. The egocentric period from three to six is a child's time to see the world only from its own position. Some persons, families, and faith groups seek to sustain such egocentricity lifelong.

The prizing of differences is the measure of maturity, just as the reverence for diversity is the mark of true spirituality.

Not a monotonous or incestuous similarity is optimal in the family, it is diversity that is desirable. The natural variety in viewpoints, differences in preferences, contrasts in perspectives, are a part of our uniqueness as human persons. They are to be prized, not feared; they are worthy of being celebrated, not despised. The hope of living in perfect security, with no differences, must die with the myth. Then the hope of security through the full acceptance of persons can be born.

Myth 3: Confrontation Is Criticism

"No matter what anyone in my family says, there's always another message that is underneath the first. Whatever is said, there is a criticism in there somewhere, and you can feel it even if you can't hear it in the words."

In families that hold this myth, all statements are suspect, all communications are received with caution. The personal implications of any comment just can't be ignored. So the listener is always on guard, ever on trial, constantly defensive. Communication becomes indirect, covert, multi-level, questioning, or concealed. The myth thus becomes a self-fulfilling prophecy. Defensiveness invites defensiveness, irritability ignites irritation. Once the cycle has begun, it rapidly becomes a negative spiral that tightens into increasing negativism.

"What was it about our family that we spoke mainly in questions? How come no one just said what they felt or thought? Why couldn't we let go and say what was going wrong between us? Didn't we trust each other with our real feelings? Couldn't we have sat down and talked it out? Why am I speaking only in questions now?"

Questions, like those just asked, become the most obvious and reliable sign of defensiveness in family communication. Questions can be used to conceal one's real intentions (I was just asking) or criticize in a covert way without taking responsibility for what was said (Why are you so defensive, can't I ask anything?) or to set up the other person with a leading question (Don't you think that . . . ?) or to catch another with trapping questions (Didn't you once promise to never . . . ?) or to punish another with whip questions (How could you do

If I Hope to Live
with No Criticism

Then one must communicate cautiously—
(Saying what one feels, frankly, is too revealing.)
One must communicate covertly—
(Asking for what one wants, clearly, is too risky.)
One must communicate in questions—
(Telling what one really thinks, openly, is too perilous.)
One must communicate indirectly—
(Speaking to another in dialogue is too dangerous.)
One must be ever on guard—
(Since one is always on trial.)
The personal implications of any message cannot be ignored.
Even compliments are covert demands,
distance and defensiveness are needed at all times.
Since (dare I say it?)—
CONFRONTATION IS CRITICISM.
(Let's hope we can live without it.)

Let the hope die.

Speaking simply in single-level statements
gives a single, vulnerable, powerful signal.
Speaking directly in personal address
frees us from reacting, frees us for responding.
Speaking openly in sharing thoughts and feelings
touches the other deeply as one is in touch with oneself.
Negative spirals of blaming and shaming
can be broken by inviting, not defending.
Positive spirals of trusting and risking
bring us into deeper and deeper understanding.
Since (I dare say it)—
CONFRONTATION IS INVITATION.

such a thing when you know . . . ?). All of these are strategies for avoiding open confrontation, but they result in creating an atmosphere of criticism.

All healthy family relationships blend confrontation and affirmation. With no confrontation they grow flabby and weak or distant and withdrawn. With too much confrontation they lose the support, caring, and bonding that affirmation alone can provide. The healthy balance of caring and candor, of loving and leveling, invite both intimacy and integrity in the relationship.

When a family is confrontation-shy, afraid of direct address, the issues do not go away, they emerge in other communications; in some families they infiltrate all other communications.

Since every statement comments on what preceded and anticipates what will follow, the possibilities for using it critically are endless. One can critique past predicaments and then punish with predictions of future failures. Or one can let go of the past and open the future.

Effective confrontation is a positive invitation to change, not a negative evaluation of the other. It is a request for growth, not a description of the other's shortcomings. It is a creative way to deepen the relationship, not a destructive means of manipulating, dominating, or rebuilding it according to one's own specifications.

The myth that all honest confrontation is criticism can be discarded. The hope for an easy acceptance that eliminates the need for dealing with the inevitable contrasts and contradictions of life must die.

Myth 4: Anger Is an Attack

"Anger? There wasn't any anger expressed in

our family. We were 'concerned' sometimes, but not angry. The unspoken rule was 'no anger allowed.' Now when I'm around anybody who loses their temper, I just have to get away as quickly as possible. It's like I can't breathe."

Destructive anger attacks, injures, seeks to destroy. It alienates the angry person as well as the object of the rage. It has few, if any, limitations since controls are the first to go when the rage bubbles up. All of us learn to fear such violence, most of us learn to control it, but some persons generalize such fear to include all anger feelings. So not only destructive rage is prohibited, the constructive and necessary anger is inhibited as well.

Constructive anger is focused on the relationship, not on the other person, on the barriers between us, not the individual. It seeks to destroy the wall of alienation, of misunderstanding, of fear that divides us, not the other person in the conflict. Such anger prizes justice between people and works to achieve it. In families that respect anger as a normal drive within persons and relationships, this energy is viewed as healthy arousal and directed toward constructive ends.

The myth that all anger is an attack turns a family conflict-shy, even deep-feeling-shy. All arousal is interpreted as anger, so when intense feelings rise—whether anxiety, fear, concern, compassion, despair or grief—it is feared because it is arousal.

"We didn't risk anything with each other. We tried to be tactful, even nice, at all times. It was like we were hoping to live without ever feeling any tension or airing frustrations; but that didn't take them away."

The hope of living with no anger and the myth

If I Hope to Live
with No Anger

Then all anger is seen as an attack,
and all anger feelings are forbidden.
So hidden anger clouds communication,
so denied anger confuses intentions,
so buried anger distorts responses,
so frozen anger deadens growth.
But who's angry? Not me!
Since (I'm not angry)—
ANGER IS ATTACK.
(Let's hope I can live without anger.)

Let the hope die.

Anger is an open expression
of aroused aliveness.
Anger is an attempt
at real contact.
Destructive anger throws up barriers.
Constructive anger breaks through walls
to restructure the relationship more justly.
Since (I'm free to feel anger)—
ANGER IS AROUSAL.

that all anger is destructive reinforce each other. They form a tight thought-loop that suppresses emotion, and confuses intentions. The hope of an angerless self, family, or circle of friends is a false hope. As it dies, the real hope of being whole in emotions and relations can be born.

Myth 5: Sadness Is Weakness

"Even when I was so broken up inside I could hardly breathe I couldn't let it show on the outside. I wouldn't give my husband the satisfaction of seeing me cry. We never let our emotions show in my family. When Mother died, Dad told us kids, 'You've got to just bite your lip and be strong.' That's what we did."

The myth that sadness is weakness and the absence of emotion is strength blinds many families to the realities of their inner lives. They learn patterns of suppressing sadness, feelings of weakness, and with these, tenderness and vulnerability. One who cannot cry wholeheartedly, cannot laugh from the soul. The person who refuses to grieve a painful loss cannot fully embrace a new happiness. To suppress sadness also represses tenderness, to freeze grief blocks also the celebration of joy.

"We lived an insulated existence with each other. Insulated. Maybe I should have said isolated. I never saw my father cry, or my brothers admit to anything but 'feeling OK.' I learned to keep my pain buried deeply."

In such "safe" families, the hope of being strong and adequate is equated with being stoic and unemotional. The reverse is true. Tenderness is power in relationship. The capacity to touch and be touched, to hear feelings and to share feelings,

If I Hope to Live
with No Weakness

Open expression of sadness,
vulnerable admission of grief,
free experience of tears,
are all seen as breaking down.
Since it exposes one to ridicule
or opens one to rejection.
So hide warm tender feelings.
Keep the armor closed.
Since (crying? who's crying?)—
SADNESS IS WEAKNESS.
(I'm biting my lip, there, I'm OK.)

Let the hope die.

Warm tenderness brings us together.
Openness and honesty invite trust.
The better you understand my feelings,
the more you will like me.
The more vulnerable I am willing to be,
the more close we can be without fear.
One need not be strong, adequate,
confident, secure at all times
in order to be respected or loved.
Since (I can let my feelings show)—
TENDERNESS IS STRENGTH.

is what bonds us to each other. Breaking through our fears with tears is not breaking down. Letting the inner reserves of passion and emotion enrich and soften reason and will, opens us to the resilience and toughness of our humanness. The hope of being untouched by pain or unmoved by sadness must die. Then the true hopes of humanness can be born.

Myth 6: Love Is Control

"How could you disobey us, with all that we've done for you? Have you no gratitude? When you know how much we love you, how could you even think of going against our wishes? If you love us, this is some way to show it!"

The anger expressed in these "loving words" betrays their real motivation. If one hopes to live with complete conformity, then loving and complying become identified; caring and conforming are seen as one. Love is control.

All family solidarity is woven from invisible loyalties that unite obligation and affection. The responsibilities that accompany parenting, husbanding, and wifing carry both duties and obligations. These must be balanced with affection and appreciation. When the two become welded into one, each no longer corrects and clarifies the other. When one is used to enforce or induce the other, love is destroyed, obligation becomes burdensome. As the two are kept separate and supportive of each other, each grows and matures.

"I was never sure whether my parents loved me or my performance. Of course it's good to be rewarded for good work, good grades, good behavior, but it leaves one feeling obliged to do it even better, or worse, to never fall short. I wanted to

If I Hope to Live
with Complete Conformity

Then love will be used
as a means to gain loyalty,
as an obligation to obey,
as a motivation to conform,
as a manipulation to shape behavior
to match the lover's goals or prescriptions
"If you love me
you will think, feel, act
as I prescribe."
Since (It's only for your own good)—
LOVE IS CONTROL.
(If you love me obey me.)

Let the hope die.

The more I love you
the more I set you free,
the more I prize you
the more I let you be what you will be.
Love sees the other
as equally worthful.
Love trusts the other
as equally well intentioned.
Love respects the other
as equally responsible.
Love values the other
as equally precious.
Since (Loving without conditions)—
LOVE SETS FREE.

know that they loved me for being me."

Love mixed with obligation becomes conditional and the recipient knows one is loved if, when, and because. The yearning to be loved as a self, for oneself, goes unsatisfied. The conditions become controlling, then stifling and devaluing.

Love that is unconditional sets free. Such love prizes the other for being, first of all, then rewards the doing. Love sees the other as equally valuable, of equal worth and preciousness. Such love values the other's free will so deeply that it refuses to invade or control. It invites rather than enforces, influences by persuasion rather than coercion, and rejoices at the other's free choices, not at perfect conformity.

The hope for uniformity or conformity must die for love to be born. The myth that love is control must be transformed by the truth that love sets free.

Myth 7: Logic Is the Last Word

"It's not that we are a family of computers, it's just that everything had to be perfectly logical. We didn't say how we felt without having a well-formulated reason for it. Facts were what was valued, a hunch or an impulsive idea were suspect. 'Think about it,' we were told, 'come back when you know your mind.'"

Logic is the last word used in a family that fears its intuitions, feelings, and hunches. The demand to be perfectly reasonable at all times attempts to eliminate the spontaneous and instinctive ways of knowing as a kind of untrustworthy craziness. Those who lose this capacity to be "crazy" and to experience their unexplainable feelings, as well as their tightly reasoned thoughts, lose touch with a major part of their inner wisdom.

"Sometimes I know something without know-ing how. I can't explain how I reached the conclu-sion, but I can feel how right it is. There's no way I can explain this to my husband. He calls it crazy, and I guess it is; but that doesn't make it false."

When conflicts must reach a logical conclusion, then people argue over the content of their differ-ences when the real issue is more often the rela-tionship. To go back and forth, 'tis 'tain't, yes, no, when the real issue is whether we feel trust, expe-rience respect, need reassurance, or are waiting for recognition, is to miss the whole point. One can be logically correct and totally wrong, perfectly rational and utterly stupid. Insight is a gift, but if it crowds out intuition it is a tyrant. Thought is necessary to maturity, but when it invalidates feel-ing it creates an invalid. Logic is the test of con-sistency and connection between ideas, but lunacy has its place to give life to relationships. Each side needs to be limited by the other, but nei-ther dare be eliminated.

The hope for objectivity alone must die. Then maturity, completeness, the balance of being a whole person, emerges.

Myth 8: Failure Is Final

"We would never have said 'winning isn't every-thing, it's the only thing' in our family. But we practiced it. We saw ourselves as winners. And there was no place in our family for a loser. So when things began to fall apart for my brother, we didn't know what to do with him. We couldn't even talk about it with each other."

The myth that failure is final, perhaps fatal, paralyzes people so that they are not free to be fam-

If I Hope to Live
with No Craziness

Then all debate
must be perfectly reasonable,
and all feelings
must have a rational justification,
and all conflicts
must be logically resolved.
Spontaneity is limited or eliminated,
impulsive responses are compulsively edited,
intuitions are discounted,
feelings forgotten or belittled.
People become correct computers.
Since (obviously, rationally, reasonably)—
LOGIC IS THE LAST WORD.
(Do I make sense or do I make sense?)

Let the hope die.

Insight *and* intuition,
thought *and* feeling,
fact *and* hunch,
logic *and* lunacy,
are all equally human,
equally necessary,
equally to be respected;
not perfection,
but wholeness;
not impeccable correctness,
but maturity
are the goals of growth.
Since (perfection is vastly overrated)—
WHOLENESS IS THE GOAL.

ily to each other. A family exists to offer the mutual help and support that all persons need whether succeeding or failing. The myth draws its power from a hope for total unbroken, unthreatened success. Or from the hope that our family can maintain a special status untouched by the vicissitudes of life.

"I feel a kind of panic inside when things go wrong, like when I lost my job. I didn't want my family to know, but I knew I couldn't keep it a secret for long. I tell myself that an act of failing does not make me a failure, but I don't feel it. When the bottom falls out of one part of my life, it feels like the whole thing has collapsed."

The connection between personal worth and performance is normal for a child in elementary school when it is hard to disconnect oneself from one's performance. But they need to be separated as one matures through adolescence until failure is seen as a behavioral problem, not a personal devaluation.

Every person needs an emotional floor of acceptance—self-acceptance, acceptance by significant others, a sense of being accepted by God—that provides a solid place to stand.

The freedom to fail is the freedom to grow. Only when one accepts the consequences for his or her choices does maturity become possible. The myth of success must be faced and dismissed before one can risk living fully. Let the hope of perfection die. The hope of being truly alive can be born.

The Myths Are with Us

Since every family is connected by hopes and myths, some healthy and freeing, some painful and binding, the first step toward growth is deep-

If I Hope to Live
without Failure

Then no errors are tolerated,
no faults dare be accepted,
no weaknesses are to be appreciated,
no immaturity is allowed.
Perfection is obviously
a minimum requirement.
Anything beyond perfection
is proof of your worth
and evidence of your gratitude
to parents, mentors, ideal self, to God.
Anything less than perfection
is the sign of being a bad person.
Since (to fail is to be a failure)—
FAILURE IS FINAL.
(Let's press toward/beyond perfection.)

Let the hope die.

Freedom to choose
is freedom to fail.
An act of failing
does not make one a failure.
The risk of living fully
includes the right to fail boldly.
Since (although it is painful)—
FREEDOM TO FAIL IS FREEDOM TO GROW.

ening awareness of the pattern they formed in the family past, the power they exert on the family present.

Every family varies from high to low investment on each of these myths, and often both poles will be represented on many of these by contrasting parents. Since they represent their own families of origin, the myths each one brings are an expression of generations of fear and trust, emotionality or its absence, tenderness or toughness.

When rating your family of origin on the scale of myths, allow yourself to reexperience the fears and the confidence, the sadness and the tenderness, the judgments and the feelings, to get beneath the myths to hopes that empower them. False hopes can be surfaced and dispelled. True hopes can be affirmed, integrated, trusted in life.

Hopes die slowly, since they rise from the deepest strata in the personality, from the earliest learnings in one's personal history, from central tendencies at the core of the self. Yet as they die, hope springs up again, born anew from the basic hope that is the basic center of the person.

The familial network of hopes is not the first and final word in the human person. Powerful as they are, they can and do, and must yield to the responsible and responsive changes of growth. Let go. Let grow.

For Reflection in the Bible

The myths of self-justification, self-preservation, self-salvation bind us to our old strategies of avoiding and evading free and open relationships in our family units.

The word which could shatter these facades of falsehood is *faith*. It is by our faith, not our per-

Rate your family of birth
on the basic myths
(Mark *M* for mother, *F* for father, *B* for both)

NICENESS IS NECESSARY	**1** 1 2 3 4 5	GENUINENESS ENABLES GROWTH
DIFFERENCES ARE DANGEROUS	**2** 1 2 3 4 5	DIVERSITY IS DESIRABLE
COMMENTS ARE CRITICISMS	**3** 1 2 3 4 5	CONFRONTATION IS INVITATION
ANGER IS ATTACK	**4** 1 2 3 4 5	ANGER IS AROUSAL
SADNESS IS WEAKNESS	**5** 1 2 3 4 5	TENDERNESS IS STRENGTH
LOVE IS CONTROL	**6** 1 2 3 4 5	LOVE SETS FREE
LOGIC IS THE LAST WORD	**7** 1 2 3 4 5	WHOLENESS IS THE GOAL
FAILURE IS FINAL	**8** 1 2 3 4 5	FREEDOM TO FAIL IS FREEDOM TO GROW

formance, that we are made whole and set free as whole persons to work out integrity in our life together. Not our perfection but our simple intention, not our achievement of maturity but our commitment to the maturing struggle with each other are the crucial elements in being "the family of God" to each other.

Reflect on this word *faith* and how it can end old hopes and set free new hoping as it is described in Saint Paul's words to the Roman Christians.

"Since then it is by faith that we are justified, let us grasp the fact that we *have* peace with God through our Lord Jesus Christ. Through him we have confidently entered into this new relationship of grace, and here we take our stand, in happy certainty of the glorious things he has for us in the future.

"This doesn't mean, of course, that we have only a hope of future joys—we can be full of joy here and now even in our trials and troubles. Taken in the right spirit these very things will give us patient endurance; this in turn will develop a mature character, and a character of this sort produces a steady hope, a hope that will never disappoint us" (Rom. 5:1-5, *Phillips*).

"By faith (not works) we are set right."

"By recognizing that we are already at peace with God, and so can be at peace with each other, we can confidently enter new relationships of grace."

"By claiming the excitement of this joy—(joy is the enjoyment of being enjoyed in right relationships before God and with each other) we can be hopeful even in the midst of conflict and tension."

"By accepting conflicts in the spirit of true

hopes, these difficulties only create a central core of patience, fortitude and perseverance."

"By maturing in such courage to live, we move toward a mature character, a character structure shaped by a steady hope, a hope which is trustworthy, which does not disappoint us."

Now review Saint Paul's words, noting the trajectory of his argument.

Faith that is claiming our preciousness as a gift of grace, not an achievement of works, sets us in right relationships that are celebrative, confident in making conflict creative, maturing in building character that is open to the future in positive, trustworthy hope.

This is a map for hope-full living for making the journey from false hopes to true hope.

Notes
1. Henri Nouwen, *With Open Hands* (Notre Dame, IN: Ave Maria Press, 1976), p. 85.
2. Shirley Luthman, *The Dynamic Family* (Palo Alto: Science and Behavior Books, Inc., 1974), pp. 119-127.

CHAPTER FIVE

HOPE DIES—
HOPE IS BORN
Hopes Dying in Depression, Born in Healing

To hope means
to be ready
at every moment
for that which
is not yet born,
and yet
not become desperate
if there is no birth
in our lifetime.

—Eric Fromm[1]

Hopes must die.

Hopes of being all-powerful, always in control,

Hopes of being all-wise, always in the know,

Hopes of being all-sufficient, always on top of things,

Hopes of being all-confident, always positive and optimistic,

Hopes of being all-successful, always first, best, ahead of the rest,

Such hopes must die before hope is born. Visible as they are in others we know, they seem invisible in ourselves until we listen deeply to the hopes that lie beneath our frustrations, within our anger, or behind any depressive feelings. At the core of our childhood experiences lie these hopes of being god-like in power, knowledge, ability, confidence, and success.

Hopelessness must die.

Hopelessness that assumes all is lost, "I have nothing to look forward to,"

Hopelessness that insists all is ruined, "I am a failure because of an act of failing,"

Hopelessness that believes that all is depressing, "I have nothing to offer, nothing of worth."

Such hopelessness must die as true hope is born. The hopelessness that rises from a depressive core in the personality must be brought to awareness and its pretentious claims that all is tragic or despairing or lost can be examined and canceled.

One personality may be filled with the grandiose expectations that emerge when hopes are expressed in ultimate language. Such hopes are framed in inclusive words—always, never, totally, completely, inevitably, invariably. And these hopes express absolute demands that completely ignore

I have been summoned
to explore a desert area
of the heart
in which explanations
no longer suffice . . .
an arid, rocky
dark land of the soul,
sometimes illuminated
by strange fires
which we fear
and peopled by spectres
which we studiously avoid
except in nightmares.
And in this area
I have learned
that one cannot truly know hope
unless he has found out
how like despair
hope is!

—Thomas Merton[2]

the realities of the adult world.

Or, for another person, the hopes are inverted, and the hopelessness is expressed in language no less ultimate, with feelings even more absolute since they are imbued with a negativism that is total, final, claiming to be terminal.

Narcissism—with its grandiosity, or pessimism—with its depressive core, occur when either pole dominates the personality. To be totally hopeful or utterly hopeless are both distortions of humanness.

Hope and Hopelessness

Part of reality belongs to hopelessness as well as to hope. There is a place for both hope and hopelessness within the whole and healthy personality. Hope claims the possibilities of the future, hopelessness recognizes its limits. In the mature person there are feelings of both, but they are kept distinct and separate. There's nothing wrong with hopeless feelings as long as they only limit, but do not contaminate the hope. Hope and hopelessness must keep separate identities within us and not permeate or dilute each other.[3]

The pretentions of safety, perfection, invulnerability must be recognized as hopeless dreams. The confidence that, although not everything will work out, all can be worked through, replaces them. And the hopeless feelings that once permeated everything else within can be contained as one side—and only one side of the soul.

With maturity should come the acceptance of limits. Not only do we need to accept our humanness with its finitude and vulnerability, we come to appreciate our limitations as individual persons. Our hopes must find their limits before they can achieve their true strength. There is nothing so strong as hope when it knows how to limit itself. In our more childish moments we hope with absolute dimensions. But not everything can be hoped for. Nothing leads to more hopelessness than the naive dream that anything can be hoped for, that everything desired is within range of hope.[4]

When one no longer clings to hopes with desperation or despair, then hopelessness can be appreciated as the sadness, grief, impotence, and despair that it is. It can be separated from the hope that remains. When hope and hopelessness are called out and strengthened, both poles begin the slow work of finding their proper place within the self. To limit hope, to limit hopelessness is the task of developing a mature inner wisdom. When one seeks to eliminate hopelessness and experience unlimited hope, a presumptuous optimism takes control of the self.

Both hope and hopelessness, both confidence and confusion, both certainty and doubt, both elation and depression, are valuable, precious, prizeworthy parts of the self. Neither dare be lost without impoverishing the self. Both must be held in creative balance, in living tension. The development of this vital balance of hope and hopelessness in the person is shaped by the presence of both of these poles in the mother and father, in the family, and in the community and society that surrounds and supports them. But hope can rise and fall as situations change, just as hopelessness can well up for periods, and then dissipate.

"However shattered an individual's hope may have been in childhood, if s/he lives in a period of hope and faith, hope will be kindled; on the other

Presumption

I know all will work out.
I will get exactly what I
want.
All is certain.
(Premature, self-willed
arbitrary optimism)

Hope is the sense of the
possible and the
confidence
that it can become
actual . . .

Hope

. . . yet is strengthened
by recognizing what is
hopeless and what can
be hoped.

Despair

I know all is hopeless.
All is useless,
changeless.
All is lost.
(Premature, self-willed
arbitrary pessimism)

Hopelessness sees
impossibilities,
feels the immensity,
understands
the futility,
struggles with
the apathy . . .

Hopelessness

. . . yet finds that not
all is impossible, futile,
final;
within the despair there
is hope.

hand, the person whose experience leads him/her to be hopeful will often tend to be depressed and hopeless when the society or class has lost the spirit of hope."[5]

The capacity to hope, the tendency of hopelessness are learned and relearned all throughout life. But certain common hopes, present in every childhood, when exaggerated, become a depressive core in the personality.

This depressive core of hopes is so thoroughly internalized by adulthood that one or all of this cluster of hopes-become-oppressive-demands would be denied if verbalized and recognized as one's own only in times of crisis honesty.

One: If I hope to be accepted I must always do my best to live up to all expectations of adults or teachers or superiors or employers, or I will be rejected.

Two: If I am to maintain respect I must avoid all tension with these important people either by doing hard work (a perfect performer) or being a goody-goody (a complete conformist) or being able to appease any irritation (a convincing placater) or I will not survive.

Three: If I am to be truly safe I must strive to regain a paradise of acceptance and security. (So I must live not for myself but for others or all is betrayed.)

Four: If I want to be loved, I must work for future love and affection. (It is not available now. It is not deserved by just being myself, but it will be available in the future if I try hard enough.) If I cannot find it, all is wasted.

Five: I can hope to succeed in all these if I fulfill all obligations and never fail. But if I do not succeed in obtaining what I want it is all my own fault. I am to blame, obviously I did not do enough, try hard enough, am not talented enough, and all is lost.

Hopelessness is fed by these consuming hopes. The all-inclusive character of their demands allows no escape. Although the dreams and aspirations attract, they do not fit the dreamer. They are beyond human reach or are attainable only at exorbitant cost. But in spite of their self-destructive nature, they can easily become a life-controlling goal.

An all-consuming goal can so captivate and dominate one's life that its frustration or failure can leave one empty, and then comes despair. Such a goal, chosen early in life, may so totally shape and control the person's development that it is the central integrating or sustaining force that keeps the self together. Although chosen originally as a way of overcoming low self-esteem or compensating for feelings of inferiority, the life goal comes to consume all else so that the person is haunted by the pursuit of an envisioned success, a desired vocation, an ideal love relationship, a grandiose picture of one's own prestige or position.

If a person has committed the whole life to being a famous actress, a Nobel Prize winner, a great minister, a professor with tenure, a mother of six children, a doctor with a successful practice, and this has become the Dominant Goal (capitalized because it has become deified) then all life is dependent on its achievement.

Unless this Dominant Goal is attained, all meaning appears faint, all happiness fades from life. The investment is so great that it alone is seen as capable of giving life significance. If a person comes to the painful realization that not even

THE PERSON WITH HOPELESSNESS AT THE CORE SEARCHES FOR ANOTHER OR A GOAL WHICH IS DEIFIED, SERVED, IDOLIZED, TO DOMINATE LIFE.

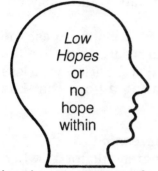

Low Hopes or no hope within

Low hope—a sense of helplessness and hopelessness— are the roots of low self-esteem. "I am worthless, powerless, helpless to change. I see myself as no good, with an inner sense of evilness, destined to failure."

High Hopes

1. A "Dominant Other" is chosen to fill the emptiness. The eagerness to please, even to live for this other, is seen as essential to life. "I must earn the other's love in order to live."

2. A "Dominant Goal" is chosen to provide the necessary meaning for life. The achievement of this goal is seen as necessary to survival. "I must achieve something great to be loved."

WHEN THE "OTHER" CANNOT FULFILL WHAT IS DEMANDED, OR THE GOAL FAILS (WHETHER REACHED OR NOT) DEPRESSION RESULTS.

becoming the famous writer, esteemed doctor, great artist, admired teacher, worshiped athlete, adulated actor, will give life its ultimate value, then the central hope that has given reason for living may disappear.[6]

If one Dominant Goal or relationship consumes a person's life, impoverishment and impairment inevitably result. That life is narrow in its experience, limited in its relationships, and dependent on a self-absorbed fantasy that would likely not satisfy in reality.

When the dream—the false hope—dies, the grieving and depression that results is not just the mourning of a lost fantasy, it is the grief over a loss of one's life lived in pursuing a hope that has proved false.

Hope and Depression

Hope has been alternately defined, when present, as the opposite of depression; when absent, the indicator of how depressed a person may be; or when acquired, the cure for depression. The relationship between basic hope and depression is complex and thoroughly interdependent.

Hope is the core element that establishes self-esteem in the person with mild, severe, or no depressiveness. Strengthening hope reduces depressiveness, losing hope increases its power, so the correlation between the two is undeniable.

If the preceding generation was known as "the age of anxiety," from the phrase in the 1947 poem by W.H. Auden, then this generation might be called "the age of depression." The often called "common cold" of mental health, depression is the most widely experienced emotional discomfort in over half the males and two-thirds the females.

Causes of Depression

IS THE DEPRESSION:
ESSENTIALLY PSYCHOLOGICAL? (Negative self-image, faulty reasoning, reality factoring)
ESSENTIALLY PHYSICAL? (Chemical imbalance in the brain)
ESSENTIALLY SITUATIONAL? (Reaction to loss, death, or stress)
ESSENTIALLY SPIRITUAL? (Emptiness, meaninglessness, alienation)

PSYCHOLOGICAL

Depressive thinking from childhood on establishes patterns of negative, passive, helpless, and hopeless views of self and the world, which then affects the brain chemistry. Thus the chemical changes in the neutral processes are rooted in or supported by the learned patterns of thinking and feeling in self-depreciatory ways.

PHYSICAL

The biological changes in the nervous system produce biochemical imbalances that affect feelings that then alter thoughts. Chemistry comes first, emotions second, thought third. If one is chemically (endogenously) depressed, one will feel depressed and will do depressive thinking.

SITUATIONAL

Sadness is a normal emotion of reaction to an external event—a loss, a death, or painful stressor. A reactive depression may follow the natural course of grief work (shock-pain-anger/guilt-resignation-acceptance). For some the grief becomes frozen, impossible. They are in a "tunnel of sorrow" with no exit, no natural resolution.

SPIRITUAL

Depressive feeling and thinking are rooted in one's sense of being alone in the universe without trust, grace, and hope. The emptiness and meaninglessness that result from this absence of basic trust of fundamental acceptance and of essential hope makes one more vulnerable to frozen grief, psychological fragmentation, and physical imbalance, since body, mind, and spirit are one.

The key issue is—What is the relationship of the capacity to hope and the experience of depression? If depression is primarily a problem of chemistry in the brain cells, then hope, as powerful as it may be, is not the necessary element. If the secret of depression is locked in the hereditary legacy from generation to generation, then hope is the effect of good genes, not the remedy for bad. If the causes of depression are locked in the childhood development, in the family pain, and in the beliefs learned, then hope has essential power to break old binds and set the person free to mature and change.

There is in modern psychiatric thinking an almost sacred respect for the view that sees the underlying problem of depression as physiological, biochemical, and constitutional in origin. The classic controversy between nature and nurture continues to be central in this debate as in many others. Both are interlocking, and no therapist dare ignore the fact that there are biological events occurring in the brain of the depressed person any more than the biological researcher can ignore that the chemical process is affected by the life experiences of the organism.

The consensus of most students of depression is that the two basic categories are psychological depression and endogenous biological depression. The endogenous depression, meaning "arising from within," emerges spontaneously with no discernible reason to explain its occurrence. When no explanation for its timing, no causation for its happening can be traced, the biological/chemical explanation seems most plausible, and antidepressant medications can offer relief from the symptoms. But most depressions combine biological, psychological, situational, and spiritual causes, and no one is able to determine with finality which one comes first, since all are interrelated within the person.

Psychological depression not only looks, feels, and responds like grieving, it is a kind of deep grief-work.

Clinical depression and normal sadness are parallel experiences at opposite ends of a continuum of painful inner feelings. Indeed, depressive illness is viewed by outstanding clinicians as an unresolved state of sorrow and sadness. The person who eventually develops a depression is someone who was prevented (in childhood) or tried to avoid (in youth) working through and psychologically experiencing a painful and psychologically overwhelming problem—a loss or the threat and fear of a loss. There was some difficulty that the person could not deal with, because in "many cases the psyche does not tolerate more than a certain amount of sadness." The individual who will one day become depressed has developed an emotional strategy early in life that is a "live now pay later" postponement of costs. By refusing to think about the tragedy or dilemma that is causing the pain, the sorrow is contained, and remains within unprocessed, unexpressed. At some point of life, external stressors or a difficult transition through one of the natural passages of development will trigger the internal sadness so that it deepens into a depression. As adolescence moves into adulthood the dormant feelings may well up. Or for the young adult whose first child turns her into a mother—a position she hates unconsciously because of the unfinished rage at her own mother's coldness or rejection—depression overwhelms

her and may become chronic until the children
have "grown and flown."[7]

In most cases the person has not a clue as to
the cause when the depressive episode occurs. The
feeling is totally, painfully conscious while the
buried hopes, fears, judgments, and rages are
repressed below the level of awareness.

Why does grief-work fail in some individuals
and depression ensue? This question is answered
differently by persons of each perspective. The cli-
nician with a biochemical orientation answers
that the causes are biochemical. The genetically
oriented researcher will note the hereditary
defects. The neurologically oriented physician will
note the cerebral malfunction. The developmen-
tally oriented counselor will chart how the person
has devised maladaptive strategies in order to survive. The spiritually oriented counselor will note
the absence of basic hope, the diminished sense of
grace, the tragic loss of meaning.

Depression and Judgments

Depression is an emotion that cloaks layer on
layer of judgments. To deeply hear these under-
layers in oneself or others requires a special kind
of listening-in-depth. Such listening recognizes
the right of the depressed person to grieve as long
as they need or choose about a loss, a failure, a
breakdown of relationship, a breakup of old
hopes. Such listening soon surfaces the judgments that are embedded in these feelings, judgments that evaluate the past, present, and future
situation, the self in worth and behavior, others
and the relationships that connect us, the wider
community and world, and even the universe and
its Creator. When depression is heavy, the judg-

ments that can be made are limited only by the energy or creativity of the sufferer; yet most of this, like an iceberg, takes place in the unconscious.

Hopeless feelings rise from the judgment that the situation is hopeless. Helpless feelings rise from the conclusion that one is powerless to change any part of the situation. Useless feelings rise from a sweeping evaluation of one's own futility.

The greatest block to effective communication with others is the ever-present tendency to evaluate. The pain of depression is exaggerated by negative evaluations out of control. The spiraling of evaluation of evaluations, of critique of criticisms, of judgments made upon the experience of judging and being judged by the self, slowly constricts the self until one is choked by the narrowing world of negativism.

Yet most of this is occurring beneath the level of awareness. The intensity of the pain, the density of the inner confusion represses any signs of the inner civil war that is taking place in the personal depths. Reclaiming these depths calls for an openness to these lower levels of the self and a willingness to own them as they rise to awareness.

The more spontaneous one can be, the more freely one's inner experience can surface and be integrated into relationships. To allow hopes, feelings, dreams to flow spontaneously is to trust the stream of one's life experience until it proves ineffective or unsatisfying. This invites a gradually increasing awareness of what is happening in one's unconscious processes. If these are destructively negative, they can be received openly, layer by layer, and directed in more healing ways.

Feelings of
Hopelessness
and
Helplessness

JUDGMENTS

"My situation is hopeless.
I have failed,
all is lost.
I am shamed,
all is exposed.
I have blown it,
all is ruined.
I am hopeless."

"My situation leaves me helpless.
Nothing I attempt
brings any relief.
Nothing I do
produces any release.
Nothing I try
reduces the pain.
I am helpless."

Ownership is the freeing step. The willingness to claim one's negative feelings, evaluations, perceptions as one's choices opens the possibility of change. Only when I can own what is happening can I become responsible; and until this takes place, the ability to respond differently is beyond my reach. The ability to change these responses is available only indirectly. Feelings do not exist apart from perceptions. As these perceptions are owned, and the evaluations canceled, the feelings change. The slowness of this process comes from the layer on layer of judgments that must be flushed out, teased out, and canceled or converted. Yet it is the necessary work of altering the depressive thinking that drives psychological and spiritual depression. Only as these destructive hopes and the judgments which express them are changed can the feelings flow creatively once more.

Depression and Instructions

In thinking, we use language in an instrumental way to instruct ourselves on what to feel, how to respond, and which hopes to pursue. Much of this language is expressed in an internal conversation we carry on with ourselves. We formulate judgments, define problems, place blame, create strategies for solving puzzles, by carrying on this running dialogue between parts of our inner self.

In depressive thinking, people tell themselves that they are inadequate, their situation is hopeless, they are helpless, their past experience is worthless, their plans are useless, their will is powerless, and nothing will change for the better. The more depressed one becomes, the more this internal use of language becomes a monologue

I. OPENNESS TO MY HOPE AND HOPELESSNESS

● *Spontaneity:* I allow my hopes to flow freely, so I feel, think, dream spontaneously. Negative feelings occur along with positive ones. I trust this stream of hopes until they prove ineffective or unsatisfying.

● *Awareness:* I attend to my hopes, thoughts, feelings to appreciate how I am experiencing myself and my world at any time. My hopeful feelings are my excited responses to a situation I perceive positively. My hopeless and helpless feelings are my responses to situations I perceive negatively.

II. OWNING MY HOPE AND HOPELESSNESS

● *Ownership:* I own my depressive feelings that spring up in reaction to my situation as my choices, my responses. The circumstances do not determine my response. The situation does not dictate my feelings. I express the hope I am able to see, feel, believe. "It" does not depress me; I make me depressed. "It" does not overwhelm my hopes. I am refusing to see the hope, choosing to feel hopeless.

● *Responsibility:* I am not directly responsible for my depressive feelings since they are chosen indirectly. I do not have the ability to respond differently with immediacy. Feelings do not exist apart from perceptions. As I (1) perceive (judge) my life situation as hopeless, and I (2) appraise (judge) myself as helpless, I (3) feel resentment-guilt-apathy-fatigue-despair-hopelessness and I (4) experience depression. So I do choose, indirectly, my depressive feelings by judging myself/my world as devoid of hope.

● *Change:* I admit I often feel hopeless/depressed before I am aware of my perceptions/judgments, evaluations and demands. Depressive feelings suggest I own my experience, take responsibility for my perceptions, state my judgments, *identify* my demands to either alter my perceptions and relate to self and other in more wholesome ways, or take action to change the situation or relationship.

and the healthful internal dialogue is cut off as one side of the self lectures the other. If this continues, self-esteem drops and the internal conversation becomes a negative commentary, like:

"How do I feel?"

"Rotten."

"Yeah, well, of course you do. Besides, look at yourself. See how you look?"

"Terrible."

"You sure do, your hair is a mess, your complexion is awful, you're too fat . . . "

"True."

"But none of that is as bad as your real problem. I mean you can't change ugliness, but . . . "

"You mean . . . "

"Do I have to remind you of how dumb you acted yesterday, of the stupid thing you said in the group and of what a schnook you were when everybody ignored you?"

Our self-concept is based, to a large extent, on (1) the capacity to maintain an inner dialogue between an affirming voice and a negative voice, (2) the ratio of the negative vs. the positive things we say about ourselves in such internal dialogues, and (3) the freedom to let the positive voice have the last word. When the two voices—as two poles of the personality—respond and balance each other, a healthful self-esteem can be constructed that takes both one's strengths and weaknesses into account. If only the positive voice is heard, there is a loss of depth, genuineness, and an awareness of finitude. If the negative voice predominates, the sense of well-being, of appropriate self-confidence and of basic self-respect are lost.

In depressive periods, the ratio of negative self-instructions and self-evaluation far outnumber

Examples of Hopeful Self-Statements

Anticipation
I am feeling a little down, I can track down what I'm doing to myself.

I will focus on what I want now, what I can do, what choices I have.

I will interrupt negative self-statements, I'll think realistically, rationally, specifically, positively.

Depression
I will deal with one thing at a time, take one step at a time, I can choose, act, think self-valuing thoughts.

This anxiety is natural, normal, neutral. I can direct it creatively.

I will relax. I am in control. I can breathe deeply. Move. Exercise.

Coping
When anxiety, fear, resentment come, I will pause, interrupt the thoughts and center in on immediate hopes.

I will keep focus on the present; on what I want to, need to, plan to do.

I will seek to limit the feelings rather than try to eliminate them.

I will not tell myself this is the worst that can happen, I can cope with it and work through it.

I will choose what I want to think about now and focus my thoughts on that.

Self-reinforcement
I keep reminding myself: "I have done it before. I was able to come through depression. I can do it again. I can face whatever comes. I can help myself, I do have hope within myself."

Examples of Negative Self-Statements[8]

Anticipation
It's starting to get to me, it will get me down.

I won't be able to think of anything but my frustration, I can't help it. I have no choice.

It will flood me with negative self-statements. I can't help thinking generally, subjectively, negatively, with total judgments.

Depression
Everything affects everything; I can't change anything unless I can change everything.

This anxiety is sick, awful, and hopelessly intolerable. I can't stand it.

I'm feeling frozen and blocked inside. I'm so tight I could snap.

Coping
When flooded by feelings, I'll fight them by adding more fears on top of fears.

I'll flee to the past—when it was good—or to the future—what will I do?

If I can't eliminate the feelings totally, they will overwhelm me.

This is the worst thing in the world. It's driving me up the wall.

I have no control over these thoughts, they just come over me; it gets me down.

Self-reinforcement
I keep telling myself, "Nothing helps. It's awful to be helpless. Nothing changes. It's terrible to be hopeless. I am helpless. I feel hopeless."

Hidden Hopes That Depress

Score—1 not like me, 0 undecided, +1 like me.

_____ 1. If I do not hope for the highest standards of achievement in my performance I will be a second-rate or a no-rate person.

_____ 2. If I do not fulfill my hopes of success I will be rejected by others, shunned and shamed by those I value.

_____ 3. If I punish myself when I have failed my hopes by reviewing them, scolding myself with them, grieving for them, I can hope to do better in the future.

_____ 4. When I fall short of my hopes I know deep inside that I am worthless, I am less of a person.

_____ 5. I hope always to perform well above average since just doing well is no satisfaction at all.

_____ 6. I hope to always be equal to or slightly better than those I admire or I am of no value at all.

_____ 7. I hope I will never need admit any fault or error openly before others because people will think less of me.

_____ 8. I hope I can immediately correct or completely change any tendency to error or failure. No one should make the same mistake twice.

_____ 9. I hope that the constant low level of anxiety I maintain to scare myself toward perfection will insure me against falling short.

_____ 10. I hope by constant review of my past actions to discover any hidden flaws to keep myself from repeating them.

the positive. Gradually they take on a more final character, and include everything in total language with an irrevocable pessimism toward the future.

Negative self-statements exercise powerful control within us through their constant repetition. The negative self-instructions are used to continuously reinstruct, in fact, to reindoctrinate ourselves in ways of thinking, feeling, and behaving. Early learned and thoroughly practiced, these instructions are self-reinforcing thought loops, self-perpetuating thought patterns that create a spiral of self-defeating messages.

Negative spirals can be reversed. The well-learned pattern can be used for its own undoing. By tracking down the negative patterns and teasing out the interlocking network of destructive self-statements, one can discover a ready-made strategy for their interruption and transformation. As a new set of hoping statements are constructed and internalized a new pattern of coping responses emerges. Scanning the old thoughts and bringing them into full awareness equips the person to recognize and to refuse them as they arise automatically. Charting new self-instructions and internalizing them by replacing the destructive thoughts as soon as they occur changes one's self-esteem and one's sense of competence.

This change from negative self-statements to positive self-instructions is not the positive thinking that denies the negative by "looking on the brighter side." This calls for discovering the negativism incorporated from childhood development, family belief systems, marital expectations, and depressive thinking styles, and owning these as the well-practiced personality patterns that have made us what we are now, but do not need to go on being.

Changing these self-instructions is not a denial of old patterns. It is a recognition, a completion, a reconstruction of personality. In changing these thought patterns, one is taking responsibility for the conscious thoughts and setting rumors of new hope afloat in the unconscious. Hopeful instructions, let loose in the psyche, can initiate changes.

Hope and Choice

The loss of hope is the loss of options. When hopelessness surrounds a person like a thick cloud of depression, it encloses, constricts, boxes in the person until alternatives disappear; there is no visible way out, no way through.

In depressive feelings, one is blanketed by discouragement or oppressed by despair so that the choices narrow down. One feels trapped, blocked, imprisoned. As the future narrows down, and possibilities are reduced, depression is increased.

In depressive thinking, one is caught in restrictive reasoning. "When I am depressed, the world seems to grow smaller, the doors around me close, the directions I can move become fewer. I can't see any way to move. That's all I can think about."

As hope returns, the possibilities broaden, the future opens again.

Hoping is closely related to the multiplicity or scarcity of options the person can see. When there seem to be few alternatives, and none of them appear workable, a feeling of hopelessness rises. Anxiety increases as options decrease, anxiety dissipates as new ways through the problem, out of the dilemma, around the obstacle, or over the dis-

Hope mobilizes.
It puts together
a disciplined surge
towards the crack
in the door of the future.
And the remarkable thing
is that time and time again
the door yields
to a determined push.
Hope springs locks
as surely as
calling a situation
"a hopeless case"
fulfills its own prophecies.[9]

couragement, are increased.

In his play *No Exit,* Jean Paul Sartre pictured hell as being in a situation with no exits, no options, no alternatives, no decisions, no freedom to choose. When all choices are gone, hope is abandoned.

When fired from a job, the stress may overwhelm the person, particularly in a setting with high unemployment. As the awareness of a variety of attractive options rise, anxiety decreases. Hope rises with the number of trustworthy directions envisioned.

Hope is imagining, choosing, trusting that there is another way.

Hope opens the options, hope welcomes the future, hope sets us free to choose again.

Hope offers tomorrow.

For Reflection in the Bible

In the midst of depressive feelings, hope seems to fade. Yet its roots lie, indestructible at the core of the person; for humans are beings of unextinguishable hope. When one is flooded by hopeless feelings, hope may seem to be totally eclipsed, yet it is never completely overshadowed, never blacked out. Even when the hopelessness has so overwhelmed the person that despair colors all thoughts and feelings, yet this underpainting of hope still shines through. Although, at times, the whisper of hope may be only the sadness that shines in the moistness of the eyes, the plaintive tone of the voice. When it appears only in the tear or the tremor it is still there as an unconscious expression of grieving, of mourning for the lost sense of preciousness, and for the inability to celebrate that preciousness openly with another. The sadness is the nonverbal witness of the inner core of the self that affirms "I am of worth (in spite of the overwhelming feelings of worthlessness that weigh me down). But I am precious in spite of it all, and I hope to feel it fully again. I do have worth (although I am only able to express it by talking of my worthlessness)."

The Psalms offer timeless expressions of hope breaking through despair. The metaphors for depression are vivid, potent, profound.

> O Lord, do not condemn me in thy anger,
>   do not punish me in thy fury.
> Be merciful to me, O Lord, for I am weak;
>   heal me, my very bones are shaken;
>   my soul quivers in dismay.
>   And thou, O Lord—how long?
> Come back, O Lord; set my soul free,
>   deliver me for thy love's sake.
>   None talk of thee among the dead;
>   who praises thee in Sheol?
> I am wearied with groaning;
> all night long my pillow is wet with tears,
> I soak my bed with weeping.
> Grief dims my eyes;
>   they are worn out with all my woes.
>   Away from me, all you evildoers,
>   for the Lord has heard my the sound of
>   my weeping.
>   The Lord has heard my entreaty;
>   the Lord will accept my prayer.
> All my enemies shall be confounded and dismayed;
>   they shall turn away in sudden confu-sion.

Psalm 6, *NEB*

Depression, experienced as the anger of God, the fear of rejection, the terror of death, causes deep sadness, grief, weariness, sleeplessness, a heaviness of soul. Yet confidence breaks out, hope rises again. Psalms 13, 22, 31, 38, 40 are rich with further symbols of depressive pain. And in each, the thread of hope is visible, the core of trust reaches out in faith and prayer. Healing comes as faith connects with the steadfast love of God. Despair is pushed back.

"The primary problem the religious counselor deals with is that of despair. The main psychological component of effective religion is hope. If the personal and organized expressions of religion are to remain in force, images, forces, and energizers of hope must continually be generated . . . . The task of effective religion, it seems to me, is to teach people how to experience the joy of life with hope."[10]

As hope moves from despair to hope, it experiences the transforming change Saint Paul reports in these contrasting words. "The burden of it was far too heavy for us to bear, so heavy that we even despaired of life. Indeed, we felt in our hearts that we had received a death-sentence. This was meant to teach us not to place reliance on ourselves, but on God who raises the dead" (2 Cor. 1:8-9, *NEB*).

"Hard-pressed on every side, we are never hemmed in; bewildered, we are never at our wits' end; hunted, we are never abandoned to our fate; struck down, we are not left to die" (2 Cor. 4:8-9, *NEB*).

Notes

1. Eric Fromm, *The Revolution of Hope* (New York: Harper & Row Publishers, Inc., 1968), p. 9.

2. Thomas Merton, "As Man to Man," *Theological Studies*, vol. 4, 1969, p. 90.

3. William Lynch, *Images of Hope* (Baltimore: Helicon Press, Inc., 1965), p. 47.

4. Ibid., p. 49.

5. Fromm, *Revolution of Hope*, p. 27.

6. Silvano Arietti, "The Power of the Dominant Other," *Psychology Today*, April, 1979, p. 57.

7. Silvano Arietti and Jules Bemporad, *Severe and Mild Depression: The Psychotherapeutic Approach* (New York: Basic Books, 1978).

8. Donald Meichenbaum, *Cognitive—Behavioral Modification, An Integrative Approach* (New York: Plenum Publishing Corp., 1977).

9. Gabriel Fackre, *The Rainbow Sign* (Grand Rapids: Wm. B. Eerdmans Publishing Co., 1969), p. 12.

10. Wayne Oates, *The Psychology of Religion* (Waco, TX: Word Books, 1973), p. 171.

CHAPTER SIX

HOPES END— HOPE BEGINS
Hopes fail us and save us in a nuclear age

Because I have confidence
in the power of truth
and of the spirit,
I believe in the future
of mankind.
Affirmation of the world and of life
contains within itself
an optimistic willing and hoping
which can never be lost.
It is, therefore, never afraid to face
the dismal reality
and to see it
as it really is.[1]

—Albert Schweitzer

There is a sense of ending in our world today, an air, a need, an ethos of ending.

Is there a word of new beginning, a word of confidence, a word of hope?

The world belongs to those who offer it a greater hope.

Hope is the most crucial emotion needed in this nuclear age.

It is needed by our children. At the period when hope is most central and crucial to growth it has been denied. Born and raised beneath the shadow of intercontinental ballistics missiles, many of our children now assume that the issue is not *if* but *when* the bombs will fall.

It is needed by our youth. At the age where hope rises most naturally, automatically, inevitably, it has been cut down. Many young people feel little hope of surviving the decade, and see marriage and children of their own as ill advised if not unthinkable. For them, the future looks like a thing of the past.

It is needed by all who seek to live on this armed and dangerous planet. As nuclear weapons multiply, the threat of annihilation increases, whether by an intentional attack, an accidental launching, or a computer malfunction. Our confidence in those who possess the power of extinction of the human race, perhaps of all life on this earth, is being stretched to the thinnest.

Every American city of twenty-five thousand or more is targeted with a nuclear device. In the event of a wholesale exchange of missiles, and once either side attacks, no other kind is conceivable, the fireball of each bomb would destroy city and country dwellers alike. At ground zero, the population would instantly vaporize. Those in shelters

would be incinerated, suffocated by oxygen deple-
tion during the fire storms, or killed by concus-
sion. In the countryside, people would begin the
slow death from fallout, from cosmic and ultravio-
let radiation due to the destruction of the ozone.
Those who survive would face a burned over world
devoid of life support systems, medical assistance,
and without immunity to the new forms of disease
multiplying in a poisonously radioactive world.

Most adults have flinched at the sound of an
explosion with the sudden image of Armageddon
flashing in their thoughts, then shrugged to recognize the reflex of fear. We have learned the language of terror in our bodies, in the slow, deep way
that creates emotional paralysis.

Hope-Work

This is the time for hope-work. Just as grief-
work brings healing to one who has suffered great
loss, so hope-work can restore faith to those who
are afflicted with despair. And certainly despair is
heavy upon all who allow themselves to think and
feel in this age of nuclear threat.

Hope-work is, *thinking the unthinkable.*

Hope-work begins with awareness, with the
recognition of things as they are. Painful as it may
be, the reality must be faced and embraced. Hope
is rooted in reality not in fantasy. Hope-work is
first the work of acknowledging our despair.

We hide from our despair.

We hide from the fear of what may befall us and
those we love. We dare not think the unthinkable,
yet we fear it may indeed come to pass. Each night
we sleep in denial of the painful reality that,
within minutes, we could be vaporized. Each day
we go about our lives without thought of the obvi-

ous, that the day could be interrupted by oblivion.

We hide from the terror of what is prepared for us. The thought of all life around us coming to an instant end, of those at a distance suffering the slow death of radiation sickness, of the earth we love destroyed as the depleted ozone layers allow the once life-giving sun to turn lethal.

Hope-work is *mentioning the unmentionable.*

The shock of putting our fears into words is so great that we hesitate to talk of what we know to be true. The conspiracy of silence is more a matter of instinctive denial than of deliberate concealment, more an automatic avoidance than it is a clear choice to join in covering the awful truth.

It is virtually impossible to carry on a conversation on the threat of nuclear war except with those who have a solid core of hope. So we hide the truth from each other and from ourselves.

We hide from the horror of what we are willing to bring about in the name of national security. When we hide from facing our nuclear preparation we not only refuse to face our imminent death at any moment, we are unwilling to face that we are potential mass killers. We are designing, building, financing, positioning, threatening, and entrusting to fallible persons and computers the weapons that can destroy the children, mothers, families of millions of human beings.

"When we hide from ourselves the immense preparations that we have made for our self-destruction, we do so for two compelling reasons. First, we don't want to face that at any moment our lives may be taken away from us. And second, we don't want to face the fact that we are potential mass killers. The moral cost of nuclear armament is that it makes all of us underwriters of the

"Nuclear war is inevitable,
says the pessimist;
Nuclear war is impossible,
says the optimist;
Nuclear war is inevitable
unless we make it impossible,
says the realist."

—Sidney J. Harris[2]

"It is sobering to remember that modern history
offers no example of the cultivation by rival powers
of armed force on a massive scale which did
not in the end lead to an outbreak of hostilities.
You are mortal men. You are capable of error.
You have no right to hold in your hands—
there is no one wise enough and strong enough
to hold in his hands—destructive powers
sufficient to put an end to civilized life
on a great portion of our planet.
No one should wish to hold such powers.
Thrust them from you.
The risks you might thereby assume
are not greater—could not be greater—
than those which you
are now incurring for us all."

—George F. Kennan[3]
Former U.S. Ambassador
to the Soviet Union

slaughter of hundreds of millions of people and the cancelation of future generations. To be targeted from the cradle to the grave is degrading. To be targeting others is degrading in a worse way."[4]

It is difficult for those concerned American Christians who decry the atheism of communist countries to face the ironic truth of our own plotting. "If the praise of God dies out in the Soviet Union, this will be the result, not of communist persecution, but of a strike with thousands of the nuclear bombs generally accepted by church-going people in the West."[5]

Hope-work is *seeing the unseeable.* The paralysis of our despair begins to lift as we visualize the future that must come if we are to survive. In seeing what is not seen, we practice hope.

What is faith? "Faith gives substance to our hopes, and makes us certain of realities we do not see," writes the author of the letter to the Hebrews (11:1, *NEB*). Hope and faith unite in visualizing what can and must be. We can see the future we are struggling, praying, striving for, and believe it into being. We can begin acting as if it were the new reality, rehearse its coming into being, act in fulfillment of it.

Human beings are visualizing creatures that exist by their ability to picture the future. We are constantly visualizing other options. To be human is to live by faith. We believe in cars, elevators, planes, traffic signals, the safety of our food, air, water, in the good will of people about us on whom we depend. In business, one must visualize budgets, inventories, strategies for five years in advance, or there is little success. In athletics one must "see" the ball going into the basket, the football between the goal posts, the puck into the net.

The sign of the nuclear age
is the Bomb.
The sign of Christ
is the Cross.
In the Cross,
all things are reconciled;
in the Bomb,
all things are destroyed.
In the Cross,
violence is defeated;
in the Bomb,
violence is victorious.
In the Cross,
evil has been overcome;
in the Bomb,
evil has dominion.
In the Cross,
death is swallowed up;
in the Bomb,
death reigns supreme.
The Bomb is the counter sign
to the Cross.
It arrogantly threatens
to undo the work
that the cross has done.
Which will hold sway in our times?

—Jim Wallis[6]

In medicine, one is taught to "see" the cancer cells destroyed, the organ healed.

Such faith has its shadow side, too. If we hold images of failure, despair, illness, destruction, or nuclear annihilation, we help, by our very belief, to bring such tragedies to pass. Of this Walter Wink writes: "That is why it is so important to take care as to what we visualize. For we are always already visualizing a future of some sort, and letting our lives be conformed to its pattern. If we believe that nuclear suicide is inevitable, then we will act, consciously or unconsciously, to speed it up."

After an address supporting the nuclear freeze, Robert Davidson, the moderator of the United Presbyterian Church, was confronted by a retired army colonel. "I oppose disarmament, it is against the will of God. What is more, the Soviets cannot be trusted."

"If we hold that view," Davidson replied, "we're liable to end by blowing each other up."

"That's right," the colonel replied, "and the sooner the better."

Take care what you believe: it may come about.[7]

Hope-work is *speaking the unspeakable.* Denial of what is taking place is rooted so deeply (it is hard for us to think the unthinkable), and fear of what may happen at any moment is so intense (it is painful for us to mention the unmentionable) that we avoid confronting, protesting, acting against death and for life. We hesitate to speak the unspeakable because we have been told that nothing else is possible.

Nothing can save us that is possible.
We who must die demand a miracle.[8]

Hope is the mood that undergirds all faith.

Each rests on the other.

Hope can have no base except in faith.

Faith cannot be sustained without the mood of hope.

Each supports the other.

Hope cannot endure without the fortitude of faith.

Hope is patient willingness to wait in faith, but it is not passive waiting.

Each is contained in the other.

Hope is active faith, choosing, moving into the future, but it does not force events.

Faith thrives on desperation. It comes into its own when nothing else seems possible.

Both empower us to act to claim the possible.

Faith is like sight. It sees the new reality, God's reality, and knows it to be true.

Hope sees the thing for which we pray as now coming, as potentially here, as a basis for present action.

Both unite in visualizing and actualizing the future.

Faith believes it into being, faith is practicing the future. Faith is living in the reality of tomorrow today.

These words by poet Wilt Auden become a credo for those who are doing hope-work. This is a struggle for hope which we simply must win. The paralysis of despair can be pushed back as we speak what is considered unspeakable. As we are confronted with the Doomsday Clock on the Bulletin of Atomic Scientists set at three minutes to midnight, we are brought face to face with mortality. We must grasp hold of the transcendent source of faith and hope in God's agenda for God's world, and speak what may appear unspeakable, to end our illusions about a nuclear safety through the threat of extinction to all living.

So hope-work leads to empowerment. The depressive despair of powerlessness is pushed back by our rising awareness as we think what was unthinkable. Ownership of our situation returns in proportion to our willingness to mention what we thought unmentionable. Action begins as we can visualize new alternatives by seeing the unseeable and results in action as we speak out with what social pressure terms unspeakable.

The silence is broken as hope returns. The status quo is not trusted when its hopes are exposed as false hopes. A new realism springs up that reclaims the future for all mankind.

False Hopes—True Hopes

Hopes that have motivated the priorities, budgets, and actions of nations and their peoples in the larger developed countries are being exposed as false hopes. These hopes are being named by many observers in every continent, and their duplicity is being found out.

Hope One: We can avoid violence by pitting

threat of violence against threat of violence. Vice set against vice produces virtue, because, beneath it, a basic humanity automatically preserves us if we allow all to go on as usual. The present situation is so desperately dangerous that it will inevitably insure our safety since no one will dare to make the first strike.

This hope is dying. The self-legitimizing character of weapons, positions, or existing situations is well known. Any policy, practice or defense posture, long enough maintained, tends to be increasingly accepted as legitimate. How quickly acts that were once judged abhorrent to all moral people can come to be seen as not only acceptable and justifiable but also laudable. Left to themselves, moral principles tend to accommodate, human values tend to become more relative, and decisions are made in ways that serve the interests of those with power. There must be a transcendent point of reference, a universal good that is grounded in more than the common human experience, to provide a corrective and a critique for our decisions and directions.

Alexander Pope described this poetically:

Vice is a monster of so frightful mien,
As to be hated needs but to be seen;
Yet seen too oft, familiar with her face,
We first endure, then pity, then embrace.[9]

Hope Two: We can trust the classic commitment to the just-war theories to safeguard us against nuclear war since by limiting warfare they eliminate unlimited nuclear exchanges.

This hope is fading fast since thoughtful people recognize that these criteria actually eliminate any possible use of atomic weapons, and thus are disregarded by the very thought of nuclear exchanges.

The seven criteria of the just-war tradition are:

1. *Last resort.* "All other means to the morally just solution of a conflict must be exhausted before resort to arms can be regarded as legitimate."

2. *Just cause.* "War can be just only if employed to defend a stable order or morally preferable cause against threats of destruction or the use of injustice." (Goals must be seen as just, the opponent must be clearly unjust, even though there is ambiguity in the self.)

3. *Right attitudes.* "War must be carried out with the right attitudes. (The intention must be the restoration of justice, not retaliation or revenge.)

4. *Prior declaration of war.* "War must be explicitly declared by a legitimate authority." (A formal declaration must precede conflict.)

5. *Reasonable hope of success.* "War may be conducted only by military means that promise a reasonable attainment of the moral and political objectives being sought." (If there is not a reasonable chance of success then it is wrong to fight no matter how just the cause.)

6. *Noncombatant immunity.* "Selective immunity must be honored for certain parts of the enemy's population" (particularly noncombatants, women, aged and children).

7. *Proportionality.* "There must be reasonable expectation that the good results will exceed the evils involved." (Thus any victory whose cost is greater than the eventual outcome expected is not right.)

How do these criteria apply to a comprehensive nuclear war? The event of an enemy launching a first strike against us could meet criteria one and two, but renders three through seven irrelevant, impossible. Thus mutual nuclear suicide would leave no room for the probability of success, the immunity of noncombatants, or any just proportionality. And the intention of restoration of justice is rendered nonsense.

The hope that the old relativism of these classic theories will aid us in an age of total war is a false hope. The true hope is that we can give up the illusions of limited nuclear attacks when we are in an age of global war. We must recognize that selective uses are impossible. It is time to lay aside such arms and build peace through interdependence.

Hope Three: We can afford to focus power, resources, wealth, technology, in fact over half of our gross national product, on the east-west conflict. It is the east-west threat in the northern hemisphere of our planet that is the central crucial problem of our age.

The real hope lies in our opening our eyes to the whole world, to see beyond ourselves and the fears we have conspired to create—conspired by locking our paranoid fears of destruction with the paranoia of the Soviet nation.

The real conflicts of our planet are north vs. south, not east vs. west. The real problem is how to aid the human tragedy, need, starvation, disease, and underdevelopment created by the overdevelopment in the north.

Willy Brandt's introduction to the 1980 report of the Independent Commission on International Development, which he chaired, graphically connects north-south issues with military spending as seen in the following:

"1. The military expenditure of only half a day would suffice to finance the whole malaria eradication programme of the World Health Organization. Even less would be needed to conquer river-blindness, which is still the scourge of millions.

"2. A modern tank costs about $1 million. That amount could improve storage facilities for 100,000 tons of rice and thus save 4,000 tons or more annually. The same sum could provide 1,000 classrooms for 30,000 children—just one tank's worth.

"3. For the price of one jet fighter ($20 million) one could set up about 40,000 village pharmacies.

"4. One-half of one percent of one year's world military expenditure would pay for all the farm equipment needed to increase food production to the level of self-sufficiency in the world's food-deficit countries by 1990."[10]

The only true hope for most of the world's inhabitants lies in the reduction and eventual disarmament of the northern hemisphere's giant nations that can lead the way toward interdependence of the world's peoples. This is the indispensable precondition to the necessary economic development. Our hope must be that the dogmas of security, the policies of economics in our own government can point in this new direction.

Hope Four: We can go on hoping that the continuing acceleration of maximal deterrence will guarantee our safety. The policies of Mutually Assured Destruction (MAD) will save us.

The hope is seductive—"If we threaten evil in order not to do it when the doing of it would be so terrible that the threat seems in comparison to be morally defensible"—if we believe this, we have

Modern man is traveling
along a road called hate,
on a journey that will bring us
to destruction and damnation.
Far from being the pious injunction
of a Utopian dreamer,
the command to love one's enemy
is an absolute necessity
for our survival.
Love even for enemies
is the key to the solution
of the problem of our world.
Jesus is not an impractical idealist;
he is the practical realist.[12]

—Dr. Martin Luther King, Jr.

been betrayed by a false hope.

The hope is arrogant—"A nuclear exchange . . . would most likely eradicate human civilization or human life itself. But Christians may be the free world's hope of remaining free, for it is we alone who can dare to risk losing much or all in a war to forestall what we consider a still greater evil, the world domination of a totalitarian, atheistic system."[11] This is the arrogance of the American officer in Vietnam who reported, "We had to destroy the town in order to save it." Now some leaders reason "We may have to destroy the earth in order to save it."

True Hopes Amid False Hopes

True hope in a time of widening hopelessness must be simply, sharply focused.

We shall not hope in our skill in negotiating from the irreversibly slippery slope of pragmatism that chooses, on the basis of who we can intimidate, what we can rationalize as for our best interest, or how we can preserve the status quo by preparation for ultimate destruction.

We shall hope in our rediscovering the priorities of human interdependence, and reclaiming the way of building national and international commitments to and covenants of peace. Nuclear war is not God's agenda for God's world. We must say it loudly, firmly, repeatedly, confidently, hopefully.

We shall not hope in continuing the we-they thinking that splits our world into camps of good/evil, righteous/unrighteous, just and justified/unjust and utterly condemned. This paranoid mind-set is not sane, not sound, whether it is the mind of an individual or the mind of a nation.

When a United States Secretary of Defense can say, "I believe that the Soviet government is every bit as dangerous to the world as Hitler," then we must recognize that whenever he thinks of the Soviet leader he sees Hitler.

We shall hope by actively loving our enemies. Enemy love is the one central spiritual task of our age. This love is expressed in both caring and confrontation. As we hope, we shall care for the welfare of all humankind by confronting with the most powerful force in the universe, truth in love. It alone endures as powerful love. Loveless power ultimately destroys itself. Powerful love given in loving power chooses the way of Jesus in refusing violence, not because it is too dangerous or too strong, but because on the scale of what really matters to God and to humanity, it is too weak.

If we live by hope, we shall hope not in great minds but in great spirits. Finally, it is not the great minds that shall save our planet, but those great spirits who are willing to pay the cost of acting, working, sacrificing themselves for peace.

Albert Einstein, a first rank mind whose thought made nuclear war possible said of the greater spirits needed, "The pioneers of a warless world are those young men and women who refuse to do military service."

If we hope for peace, for life, for shalom we will join the great spirits who dream dreams of peace, and give themselves to bring those dreams to reality.

This is the time to let false hopes die. We are tortured by the false hopes of violence and armaments that have divided and decimated our populations generation after generation. All hopes that are anti-shalom must be seen for what they are,

I have a dream that one day
this nation will rise up
and live out the true meaning
of its destiny—to create harmony and peace.

I have a dream that one day
the greatest arms producer for the world
will turn its creativity from the weapons of war
to the work and preparation of peace.

I have a dream that my children
will one day live in a world
where they will not be safe because of terror
but secure because of trust among all people.

So let peace roll down . . .
from the mighty mountains of America.
Let peace roll down
from the Ural Mountains to the Steppes of Russia.
Let peace roll down
from the Mongolian Mountains of China.
Let peace roll down
from the Himalayas of Asia.
Let peace roll down.
When we let it roll, we will speed the day
when all God's children, black and white,
collective and individual, socialist and capitalist
shall join hands and say, "Peace at last.
Thank God almighty, peace at last."

After the speech to the
Washington March, by
Martin Luther King, Jr.

though they come among us dressed in shalom clothing.

Shalom is the will of God, shalom that brings an end to brother lifting the sword against brother, of neighbor seeking to destroy neighbor. On this small planet there are only brothers, sisters, and neighbors left. There is no one else. And those we have seen as enemies are to be loved, not destroyed, and their welfare regarded with care, not rejected in hate.

The way of Jesus is the way of shalom. His way can be, must be, our way too.

For Reflection in the Bible

Shalom is the wholeness of life in its fullest and most complete God-given maturity; peace, justice, righteousness, truth, love all unite in this vision of the age God has promised us.

The gospel is a gospel of shalom (Eph. 6:15). The God who proclaims this gospel is a God of shalom (1 Cor. 7:15; 2 Cor. 13:11). The Messiah who brings in the messianic age is simply named "Shalom" (Isa. 9:6; Mic. 5:5; Eph. 2:14). The goal of all God's working, luring, loving, is the establishment of a kingdom of shalom (Luke 2:14; Rom. 14:17; John 14:27; Eph. 1:2-14).

The way of shalom is the way of Jesus. The only way in which we are called to imitate His example is in the pursuit and practice of shalom (1 Pet. 2:20-25).

When we despair that God's shalom will not finally triumph we are joining the forces of anti-shalom. Even when one's own age is filled with tragedy and one's own life is marked by suffering, one can continue to hope; in fact, one must hope if the inner urgencies of faith are not squelched.

Tragedy is not the final word, injustice is not the end, suffering is prologue, not the concluding word. No obstacle, not even death, will ultimately silence the forces of creativity and redemption in this universe. As Saint Paul shouts in explosive faith:

"Then what can separate us from the love of Christ? Can affliction or hardship? Can persecution, hunger, nakedness, peril, or the sword? 'We are being done to death for thy sake all day long,' as Scripture says; 'we have been treated like sheep for slaughter'—and yet, in spite of all, overwhelming victory is ours through him who loved us. For I am convinced that there is nothing in death or life, in the realm of spirits or superhuman powers, in the world as it is or the world as it shall be, in the forces of the universe, in heights or depths— nothing in all creation that can separate us from the love of God in Christ Jesus our Lord" (Rom. 8:35-39, *NEB*).

Yielding to despair is surrendering to hell. Hell, the final consequence of sin, is existence drained of all hope. In *The Divine Comedy*, Dante pictures this graphically by inscribing over the entrance to hell the words *"lasciate ogni speranza, voi ch'entrate.* Abandon all hope, ye who enter here."

Hoping is seizing the promise of heaven. Heaven is the guarantee of eternal shalom. It is the certainty that the universe is on the side of justice and the last word is with God, not with humanity; and God's last word is shalom.

Notes

1. Albert Schweitzer, *Civilization and Ethics* (London: A & C Black, 1923), p. 169.

2. Sidney Harris, in Mary Lou Kownacki, *A Race to Nowhere* (Chicago: Pax Christi, 1980), p. 11.

3. George Kennan as quoted in *Evangelical Newsletter*, February 20, 1981, p. 1.

4. Jonathon Schell, *The Fate of the Earth* (New York: Alfred A. Knopf Inc., 1982).

5. Dale Aukerman, *Darkening Valley* (New York: Seabury Press Inc., 1981), p. 141.

6. Jim Wallis, *Call to Conversion* (New York: Harper and Row Publishers Inc., 1981) p. 88.

7. Walter Wink, "Faith and Nuclear Paralysis," *The Christian Century*, May 3, 1982, p. 235.

8. W.H. Auden, *For the Time Being, A Christmas Oratorio* (New York: Random House Inc., 1976).

9. Alexander Pope, source unknown to author.

10. Alan Geyer, *The Idea of Disarmament* (Elgin, IL: Brethren Press, 1982), p. 164.

11. Harold O.J. Brown, *Eternity*, June 1980, pp. 16-17.

12. Martin Luther King, Jr., Source unknown to author.

BIBLIOGRAPHY

Augsburger, David. *When Caring Is Not Enough.* Ventura, CA: Regal Books, 1983.

Beachey, Duane. *Faith in a Nuclear Age.* Scottdale, PA: Herald Press, 1982.

Erikson, H. Erik. *Insight and Responsibility.* New York: W.W. Norton & Co., 1964.

_____ . *Identity, Youth and Crisis.* New York: W.W. Norton & Co., 1968.

Fackre, Gabriel. *The Rainbow Sign.* Grand Rapids: Wm. B. Eerdmans Publishing Co., 1969.

Fromm, Eric. *The Revolution of Hope.* New York: Harper & Row Publishers, Inc., 1968.

Geyer, Alan. *The Idea of Disarmament.* Elgin, IL: Brethren Press, 1982.

Kraybill, Donald. *Facing Nuclear War.* Scottdale, PA: Herald Press, 1983.

Lynch, William. *Images of Hope: Imagination as Healer of the Hopeless.* Notre Dame, IN: University of Notre Dame Press, 1974.

Moltman, Jürgen. *Theology of Hope.* New York: Harper & Row Publishers, Inc., 1967.

Muyskens, James L. *The Sufficiency of Hope.* Philadelphia: Temple University Press, 1979.

Schell, Jonathon. *The Fate of the Earth.* New York: Alfred A. Knopf Inc., 1982.

Sider, Ronald and Taylor, Richard. *Nuclear War and Christian Hope.* Downers Grove, IL: InterVarsity Press, 1982.

Wallis, Jim. *Call to Conversion.* New York: Harper & Row Publishers, Inc., 1981.